WRITE ON: A CONFERENCE APPROACH TO WRITING

D0825953

WRITE ON:
A CONFERENCE APPROACH TO WRITING

JO-ANN PARRY
DAVID HORNSBY

Contributors to original report:
Don Stott
Mary McDonald
Maryanne Thorpe
Claire McInerney
Cheryl Reid
Heather Littlejohn

Heinemann
Portsmouth, NH

Heinemann Educational Books, Inc.
70 Court Street, Portsmouth, NH 03801
Offices and agents throughout the world.

Copyright © 1985 by Jo-Ann Parry and
David Hornsby
First U.S. edition published 1988.
10 9 8 7 6 5 4 3 2 1

Library of Congress Cataloging-in-Publication Data

Parry, Jo-Ann.
    Write on: a conference approach to writing/by
Jo-Ann Parry, David Hornsby; contributors to the
original report, Don Stott . . . [et al.]. — 1st U.S. ed.
    p.   cm.
    Bibliography: p.
    ISBN 0-435-08460-7
    1. English language — Composition and
exercises — Study and teaching (Elementary)
I. Hornsby, David. II. Stott, Don. III. Title.
PE1404.P37 1988
372.6'23 — dc19   87-22929
                                              CIP

Printed in Australia by Globe Press Pty Ltd

CONTENTS

PREFACE

The original Task Force team's report titled 'A Manual for the Writing Teacher' proved to be very popular with teachers, as the members of the Task Force hoped it would be.

The research was begun in 1980 and the report was compiled over a period of three years. As a result of requests for the report, it was decided that a more complete text should be written. This decision was made because:

1 The research and documentation covered a four year period and needed updating;
2 Some classroom organizational issues have since been refined;
3 More recent research further supports and clarifies some of the ideas which were discussed in the original text and has substantiated the links between reading and writing;
4 During our work in schools since the report was published, we have had the opportunity to gain further insight and a broader perspective of writing classrooms in operation.

The major changes include:

1 sections of Chapter 3, including introductory activities, planning in work programs, and publishing children's work;
2 sections of Chapter 5, including organization issues, planning in the infant school;
3 a new chapter on spelling;
4 a new chapter on the links between reading and writing;
5 a new chapter on a conference approach to reading which discusses organizational issues which strengthen the links between reading and writing.

There are many issues to do with reading which warrant further discussion. Chapter 10 on reading is purposely brief, but the conference approach to reading is discussed in length in a companion volume.[1]

We thank the School of Education at La Trobe University for releasing the original report, but we would particularly like to thank the members of the Task Force team for trusting us to re-write and extend the text.

The book is meant to be practical; little theory has been presented. For those who wish to consider theoretical positions more carefully, further reading lists are provided at the end of each chapter and a substantial annotated bibliography of journal articles is included at the back of the book.

We hope that teachers *do* find this a practical book.

Special thanks to Don Stott for his extra efforts in compiling the original report.

Thanks also to Marjie Tkatchenko for allowing us to reproduce her room plans, and to Alan Jager and the children of Reservoir East Primary School for the photographs.

---

1. Hornsby, Sukarna & Parry, *Read On: A Conference Approach to Reading*, Martin Educational, 1986

1 PREPARATION

Before you begin any new program you need to think carefully about your reasons for adopting the new approach. Taking on a new program simply because it is fashionable or 'looks O.K.' is rarely successful. It is important that the teacher sees a need for a change and agrees philosophically and theoretically with the approach, as well as finding it a practical proposition.

We hope the following program will be as exciting, stimulating, and rewarding for you as we have found it to be. However, before you launch yourself head first into a flurry of activity, there are several important factors to consider.

The quickest way to give yourself a nervous breakdown is to attempt too much too soon. Take each stage slowly, and make sure you feel confident with what you are doing before you move on to the next stage.

One way for both you and your class to survive may be to start with a small group of children who are not averse to writing. However, some teachers prefer to begin with the whole class rather than with small groups. The choice is the teacher's — there is no right way.

If you have introduced a new organization for spelling or any other part of your program, then keep it. Obviously if you have a technique with which you feel very comfortable, you would be crazy to throw it out. Find a way to include it within the new program.

The following points are designed to help get you thinking about the 'process approach' to language development. And then you will be able to make an informed decision as to whether or not this approach is really for you.

One Way to Begin a Writing Program

1 Read
Make sure you have a good understanding of the writing research findings.

Suggested reading — Any Primary English Teaching Association (P.E.T.A.) publication, 'Writing Process Laboratory Papers', titles listed in Further Reading at the end of this chapter and relevant titles listed in the Bibliography.

2 Discuss
- If possible, discuss the program/approach with a teacher who is currently using it.

- Visit the grade/school and see the program in operation.

- Attend inservice training if available or invite a language consultant or support person to discuss the approach with you.

3 Begin Group 1
- Begin the program with a small group of children (preferably independent workers).

- Carefully explain the main features of the program to these children. Try to hold a session every day. Issue writing folder and explain the records.

- **Do not try to explain everything at the beginning**
As the children begin to edit, revise, and rewrite, work through these aspects with them.

- Work with just one group until they have completed their first writing piece and have begun their second (1-2 weeks).

- Accept all efforts.

10 Other teachers
- It is important to discuss with other teachers around you (co-ordinator, grade level) what you are doing. You will find it easier if two or more grades start the program. Being able to talk out advances, activities and problems makes introducing the program easier.

9 Outside help
- If classroom assistance is not possible, then consider seeking parent assistance in bookmaking, typing (home and at school) and display.

4 Difficulty
At first you will have most of the children at the same stage of writing. That is, they will all finish their first draft at roughly the same time. This is a difficult period. Stagger individual or group conferences. As the children grasp the process they will soon space out and be at different stages of writing, and their demands on you will decrease.

5 Begin Group 2
- As the first group gains confidence in the process and understands the organization, introduce a second group.

- Use the first group to explain the organization ('peer-age tutors') to the second group.

6 Publish
- Move fairly quickly to 'publishing'. It is important that the children see that their writing is for a real audience.

- Produce a class book with some of the stories typed in. Publications at this stage need not be grand.

- Read finished stories to group.

7 Further groups
- Once the second group has settled into the approach, introduce another group.

- Repeat the procedure until the whole class is involved.

8 Assistance
- Seek assistance in the classroom to help with conferencing, working with individuals etc. from support teachers, teacher aides, consultants, parents, cross-age tutoring.

- It is important that whoever helps you also understands the process and organization involved. Detailed discussion needs to take place to develop a team approach.

What a Teacher Should Know

Questions to ask before beginning a writing program

1 What do I know about the writing research findings? What are the implications?
2 What would be my objectives for the program?
3 Am I prepared to let the children take control of topic choice and ownership of their writing?
4 What do I know about my children's interests?
5 What could be the possible organizational changes needed to run the program (i.e. if children write everyday)? (Timetabling, work program, storage and display, writing centre, room organization, class seating — individual or group arrangements.)
6 What about the existing language program? How would this approach to writing fit in with it?
7 Would this approach be acceptable to the administrators and other teachers with whom I work?
8 How would I structure conferences and small teaching groups (as mainly individual, small groups, the whole grade or a combination of above)?
9 How do spelling, punctuation and grammar fit in with this writing approach? How would I teach them?
10 What parts of my existing language program should continue while I introduce new classroom procedures? (E.g. establishing conference procedures would be a higher priority than attending to new spelling procedures.)
11 What records would I need to keep which would be practical and useful in developing teaching strategies?
12 How would I evaluate:
   (a) the program?
   (b) the children's progress?
   (c) my performance?
   (d) the evaluation process?
13 What (new) materials/resources would I need? How could these be effectively organized?
14 How should I inform parents of the program? How could I enlist their support?
15 What would be my first important priorities in making changes? Will these changes serve the needs of the child?

Further Reading

Allen, R. & Allen C., *Language Experience Activities*, Houghton Mifflin Co., Boston, 1976.

Beavis, C., *Writing P-12*, Education Department of Victoria, 1983.

Hill, Kathleen, *The Writing Process*, Nelson, 1984.

Fleet, A. & Martin L., *Thinking It Through*, Nelson, 1984.

Graves, D. H., *Writing: Teachers and Children at Work*, Heinemann Educational Books, 1983.

2 WRITING WORKSHOPS

Writing *is* a process. We don't need to refer to a 'process approach' to writing: the terminology is redundant. By referring to a 'process approach' there is the possible inference that it is a particular 'method' of teaching writing or that there is a set procedure or series of steps to follow. When children write, they *are* involved in a process whether teachers recognize it or not.

The flowchart following (see page 6) is an attempt to organize the elements of writing which need to be considered and where writers may need help. It is not to be interpreted as a blueprint for procedural steps that every child will follow.

The elements are integral to writing. However, they are not always overtly demonstrated or observed, even when they are taking place in the classroom. For example, many aspects of rehearsal occur outside the classroom. This happens with all writers, including adults. A person may hate the job of cleaning out the spoutings and will put it off for months. But the same person, when he or she has an essay to write, will gladly spend all day on the roof cleaning out the spoutings! However, at the same time, she or he is thinking 'Maybe I should just get that extra reference at the library this afternoon', or 'I should leave that part for the conclusion', and so on. In other words, that person is rehearsing for writing.

Other elements of the writing process will also go unnoticed. Revisions may be made away from the writing (away from the pen and paper). What needs to be understood clearly is that:

1 rehearsal (pre-writing) is not necessarily 'Draft 1';
2 writing (drafting/revising) is not necessarily 'Draft 2'.
3 post-writing/publishing is not the 'good copy' or the second draft simply re-written in the writer's best handwriting.

There is not a set number of drafts; there is not a recipe to follow. Drafting is not synonymous with re-writing. To re-draft, the writer does *not* necessarily have to re-write. Three or four drafts may be seen on the one piece of paper.

Revision, or 're-seeing' a piece of writing, is often required, but there are also occasions when little or no revision takes place. If a child has a topic that is really working well, little change may be needed. A child in the first year of school will rarely revise. 'Just the miracle of putting down information in words is sufficient to fulfil their intentions.'[1] Sometimes, the topic itself is not worth pursuing and the writer will not waste time revising.

Teachers need to look at each individual writer, and what's more, each writer will demonstrate different writing behaviours with different writing tasks. A writer may work through several drafts on one piece, but in the very next piece, may only write one draft before it is ready to be 'published'.

The Writing Process

Experience
idea or incubation
Perhaps I could write about that?

Rehearsal (pre-writing)
- discussing
- researching
- scribbling
- drawing
- interviewing
- note-taking
- constructing

Writing
- reductive/rough
  - drafting
  - revising (adding, deleting, re-ordering, re-seeing)
  - editing
  - rewriting
  - proof-reading
- substance/polished

Post-writing
- appropriate format despatched to readers

Audience feedback
- a response that is conveyed to the writer

---

1. Graves, D., *A Researcher Learns to Write: Selected articles and monographs*, Heinemann Educational Books, 1984

Dimensions of Writing

Four dimensions of writing to be considered are:

1 function   3 purpose
2 mode   4 form

Teachers need to keep in mind a wide range of writing experiences in which children should be involved. It is a common misconception that children are only required to write in personal narrative in 'writing classrooms'. Function, mode, purpose and form need to be considered. It may be useful to take the following summaries as a starting point when attending to the many dimensions that constitute writing development. The original sources should be consulted for more detail.

Function

Britton[2] describes three major functions:

Personal	Transactional	Artistic
(expressive)	(practical)	(poetic)

- Personal writing tends to be loosely structured and free-flowing; the focus is on the writer.

- Transactional writing demonstrates an interaction with the world by writing in a practical way. The focus is on the information to be conveyed.

- Artistic writing expresses ideas. The focus is on the language itself and its structure.

Mode

Common modes of writing include narration, description, exposition, analysis, argument, persuasion, evaluation and discourse.

Moffett[3] refers to four modes of writing: narration, description, exposition and argument. Murray[4] refers to genres and lists them as fic-

---

Language activities

Nature of activity is determined by need of the writers, at the time, or the Teacher's Weekly Focus. Across-the-curriculum activities such as drama, poetry, discussion, music, teacher writing/modelling.

Conferences

Nature and focus of conference changes with the age of the children, their stage as writers and the number of their draft. Emphasis is *always* on what the *writer* has to say. The teacher's role is that of active listener.

Small teaching groups

These deal with the mechanics of writing such as punctuation and grammar, or other special issues as they arise. Small-teaching groups are held when the need is demonstrated by the writers or their work.

Publishing (Sharing)

- book production
- exhibitions
- oral
- display

Note: The process is recursive, not linear.

---

2. Britton, J. *Language and Learning*, Penguin, 1970

---

3. Moffett, J., *Teaching the Universe of Discourse*, Houghton Mifflin, 1968
4. Murray, D., *Learning by Teaching*, Boyton/Cook, 1982

tion, poetry, personal narrative, familiar essay, argument and exposition. Boomer[5] refers to genres and styles.

The terminology is not consistent; different authors use different terms for much the same thing. What is important is that teachers are aware of the different dimensions of writing.

Purpose and form

Purpose and form deal with a wide range of possibilities available to the writer. The following list shows how purpose and form are closely linked and provides teachers with a useful framework. Such a framework must be considered with the function of the writing and the intended audience.

Function, mode, purpose and form are all inter-related. In seeking working definitions, we have found no distinct or precise statements which allow separate descriptions of these dimensions of writing. They *are* interrelated and dependent upon each other.

Purpose	Writing form[6]
To record feelings, observations etc.	• Personal letters • Science reports • Poems • Jottings of sensory impressions from observations, stories, drama, music, art • Diaries, journals
To describe	• Character portraits • Reports of a sequence of events • Labels and captions • Advertisements, e.g. wanted to buy or sell, lost and found
To inform or advise	• Posters advertising coming events • Scripts for news broadcasts • Minutes of meetings • Invitations • Programs
To persuade	• Advertisements and commercials • Letters to the editor • Notes for a debate • Cartoons
To clarify thinking	• Note-taking for research topics • Explanations of graphs, science diagrams, etc. • Jottings
To explore and maintain relationships with others	• Letters • Making requests • Greeting cards • Questionnaires
To predict or hypothesise	• Speculations about probable outcomes in health, science, social studies topics • Endings for stories • Questions for research or interviews
To make comparisons	• Charts • Note-making • Diagrams, graphs • Descriptions
To command or direct	• Recipes • Instructions, *How to make a* • Stage directions • Rules for games, safety, health, etc.
To amuse or entertain	• Jokes, riddles, puzzles • Scripts for drama, puppet plays • Stories and poems • Personal anecdotes

5. Boomer, G., 'Towards a Model of the Composing Process in Writing', paper presented at the ANZAAS Conference, Adelaide, 1980

6. 'Writing: R-7 Language Arts', Language Arts Committee, Education Department of South Australia, 1979

Introductory Pre-writing Activities

The most successful writing classrooms are rooms in which children are encouraged to experiment with all forms of expression — drama, music, dance, art/craft — not just writing. These forms of expression, which result from visual, auditory and tactile stimuli, are just as important as the written forms of expression.

In addition to this, a successful writing classroom functions best when it becomes a 'writing community'. We must help children to realize that although writing is basically a solitary activity, they are surrounded by writers who are able to help and give support whenever needed. We cannot expect children to 'open up' and share their writing unless they feel secure within the 'writing community'. It is one of the teacher's major roles to create and maintain this secure, supportive environment.

To help children express themselves in different ways and to develop the 'writing community', it is important to begin each writing session with a pre-writing or introductory session. This session will often take 10 to 20 minutes, regardless of year level.

Note: 'pre-writing' does *not* refer to the exercises and activities traditionally completed before practising handwriting skills. Writing means composing, so pre-writing activities are activities which help children before they begin to write/compose.

It must be stressed that these introductory sessions are *not* motivational sessions to get children to write about something. For example, if an introductory activity consists of the class interviewing a local resident about what the school was like when he or she attended it 50 years ago, the intention is *not* to have all the children write about the school 50 years ago! Rather, the intention is to have them learn something about interviewing techniques that may help them to collect information for their own writing topic. 'A kid can spot a motivation at a hundred paces.'[7] Given a secure writing environment, children do not require motivation, and may in fact resent it!

The major purposes of introductory, pre-writing activities are:

1 to foster the sense of 'community';
2 to help children clarify ideas, explore approaches to and ways of handling a topic, compare individual approaches to a single experience;
3 to help children talk and learn from, and about, each other.

Introductory, pre-writing sessions also help the children to see the link between all areas of language. The children realize that reading, writing, speaking and listening are not unrelated blocks of time during the day. The sessions also help children understand the purposes for writing and they, like adults, perform much better when they have this understanding.

Typical pre-writing questions might include:

1 Am I worth listening to?
2 What do I have to say?
3 What information do I have to communicate?
4 What really happened?
5 How shall I begin?
6 What questions will my reader need answered?

Introductory, pre-writing sessions can be roughly categorized into three groups. These groups are for convenience only; in many cases there will be an overlapping of activities.

1 Community activities
2 Expressive activities
3 Writing strategies

1 Community Activities

(a) Music
 i group singing
 ii changing words to songs
 iii action songs
 iv percussion band
 v dance

(b) Drama
 i group role-play
 ii group mime and movement

(c) Literature
 i poetry recital

GRADE 3 C ✿✿

HOBBIES

Allen – stamps
Angela – b.m.x
Bianca – horses
Bruce – cooking
Douglas – cars
Esther – photography
Emilio – gardening
Freddy – fishing
Gail – fishing
Huan – telling jokes
Ilsa – drawing
James – swimming

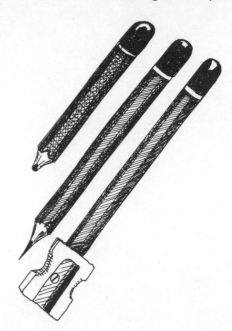

ii dramatizing favourite part of a story
iii group story-telling
iv serial reading
v story-telling (by teacher, children, visitor, etc.)

(d) Teacher writing
The teacher displays a draft of a story she or he has written. The group discusses the draft and the revisions.

(e) Group writing
wall stories

(f) Sharing of expertise
i Children should be aware of strengths among their own ranks. The community introductory sessions can be used to promote this awareness through talks by children about their hobbies, skills and experiences.
ii Children should be encouraged to bring along tangible pieces of their lives to share with others (photos, souvenirs, collections, etc.)
iii Children should learn how to interview other children about their areas of expertise. This may include their 'expert' knowledge of a character from a book, and they can role-play the character.

(g) Sharing of writing concerns/issues
What kind of a writer are you?
Talk about the differences between writers.
i The 'splurger'
— who writes straight away and tries to get everything down on the page before looking back
ii The 'agonizer'
— who thinks things out in the head before writing
iii The 'backtracker'
— who goes back to check each sentence before writing a new one.
Are there any other kinds of writers?

2 Expressive Activities
(a) Music
i appreciation/listening activities
ii painting in response to music (following the flow of the music)

(b) Literature
i 'zoning in' on ways particular writers say things
ii responding in personal ways to particular pieces of literature which have had a personal impact

(c) Drama
  i individual mime/role-play activities
  ii dance and movement

(d) Tactile experience
touch and describe, imagination exercises

(e) Different media
  i drawing an incident or setting to clarify detail or content
  ii modelling using clay, plasticine, play dough
  iii construction using Lego, blocks, boxes, etc

3 Writing Strategies
Activities to do with writing strategies are those which help the children develop the 'writers craft'.

The introductory session can be used for:
- discussions on 'getting started'
- ideas about choosing topics
- ways of writing/editing
- making links with reading
- ways of 'collecting and connecting' information

(a) Choosing topics/getting started
  i Brainstorming — don't assume that children know how to 'brainstorm'. Do one in class on the chalkboard, e.g. 'What is red?' or 'What would happen if . . . (rabbits were as big as people)?'

Brainstorm topics for writing. List general topic areas on the chalkboard, e.g. accidents, holidays, birthdays, celebrations, families, pets, etc.

Make the topics more specific, e.g. 'My Trip' (to Phillip Island) 'Camping' (Eildon — the kangaroos I saw) 'Trucks' (when I went for a ride with my uncle).

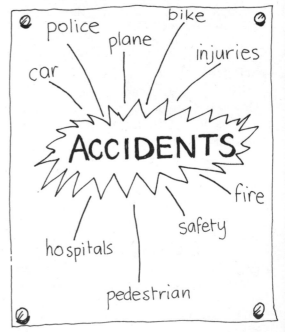

ii Working with partners
- Encourage children to *think* about their topic and then discuss it with a partner.
- an interview with a partner sometimes helps discover new topics, e.g. 'This is your life!'
- develop the idea of **choice**. Talk with children about choosing the best or most appropriate options.

iii Interviews
- The class or a panel of children could interview a teacher, the principal, a visitor, a member of the community, etc. Preparation of the questions beforehand is important.

iv Discussion groups
- Give the children opportunities to talk in small groups about self-chosen topics. The importance of talk must not be forgotten.
- To progress from 'talk only', ask the children to jot down on small pieces of paper the things they talked about. When several pieces of paper have been completed (after several free talk sessions), the pieces may be stapled together or attached to a larger piece.

transfer to list of
"Things I might write about"

- As a whole class, or in groups, the children are then encouraged to circle the two or three topics which they think they know most about, or those which interest them most. These become possible writing topics which can be added to the ever-growing 'Things I Might Write About' list inside the front cover of the writing folder (see page 40).

(b) Developing confidence to put pen to paper
  i diaries, personal journals
  ii written brainstorms
  iii written conversations: Partners hold a 'conversation' by writing down their speech. There is no talking, e.g.
  A: 'Hi.'
  B: 'Hello.'
  A: 'What are you doing at lunch-time?'
  B: 'I want to play four-square. Do you?' etc.
  iv jotting down of sensory impressions:
  - all the sounds heard in 15 seconds
  - everything seen from the art room window
  - how the first night at camp felt.

(c) Expanding language models and developing an interest in words
  i Conduct a whole class session on transforming, reducing and expanding sentences. As often as possible, use the children's writing as a model on the chalkboard or overhead projector. Use strategies such as those suggested in the *Sounds of Language* teachers' manuals.[8]

  Also use extracts from well-known children's literature, e.g.

There was an old $\begin{bmatrix} \text{woman} \\ \text{witch} \\ \text{worm} \end{bmatrix}$ who lived in $\begin{bmatrix} \text{a shoe} \\ \text{a ditch} \\ \text{the dirt} \end{bmatrix}$

Baa baa black sheep have you any wool?
Grunt grunt dirty pig have you had a wash?

  ii Big books and shared-book experience — the Ashton Scholastic *Read It Again* series and similar 'big books' are very useful for sharing language models with children. The *Read It Again* teachers' manuals and addi-

---

8. Martin, Bill jnr., *Sounds of Language* series, Holt, Rinehart and Winston Inc., 1970

tional teaching notes are most useful and offer many practical suggestions. A useful text is Holdaway, *The Foundations of Literacy*, Ashton Scholastic, 1979.

iii Oral cloze activities — Use oral cloze to help develop word choice and discuss alternative words. It can be done by reading a short story with a predictable structure. (Again, the *Sounds of Language* books (Holt, Rinehart and Winston) are excellent; also the *Storybox* materials by Rigby.)

iv Poetry — Read a poem which uses imagery or portrays strong feelings. Discuss word choice with the class and relate the children's use of words in writing.

v Word usage — Find and list better words for adjectives such as good, nice, big, small, etc.

Pin up lists of words in categories that help children say and write their observations and feelings with more depth (e.g. colour words, shape words, sound words, taste words, rhyming words, similies, metaphors, etc.). Keep the lists open so that additions can be made.

vi Word wall — A word wall to hold lists of words is useful. It can include high-frequency words which occur in the children's own writing.

A focus for introductory activities

So that shared pre-writing activities are not ad-hoc, it is useful to work a weekly focus into the planning of the writing workshop. The focus will usually come from one of the three broad areas already outlined. One week, the focus may be on a particular author's work, the following week on ways of collecting information and the week after on music. There is no limit to what may be chosen as the weekly focus.

Through any weekly focus, all areas of language — listening, speaking, reading, writing and thinking — can be attended to.

As can be seen, the focus will often be linked with other curriculum areas.

Example 1 — Focus: Ted Greenwood (author/illustrator)

Monday	Listening	Extracts of his work are read by the teacher.
Tuesday	Speaking	In small groups children discuss the pros and cons of text/illustration matching.
Wednesday	Reading	Children choose from a selection of his books.
Thursday	Writing	Children write their impressions about the kite in 'Obstreperous' (individual or small group work).
Friday	Writing	The teacher records personal feelings on an overhead transparency. Collective pooling of ideas should be encouraged.

Example 2 — Focus: Collecting information

Monday	Writing	The class goes for a 10-minute walk around the school and lists key features of the school environment that are observed.
Tuesday	Talking/Listening	The principal is invited to be interviewed about the school environment.
Wednesday	Reading	The children work individually or in small groups, collecting information about buildings, gardens, sports facilities, playground equipment, etc.
Thursday	Talking/Listening	Small groups of children discuss the information collected on Wednesday.
Friday	Writing	The children write about one aspect of the school environment which is good and/or needs improvement.

Example 3 — Focus: Music (songs e.g. nursery rhymes)

Monday	Listening	Children listen to selected songs on tape/record. The teacher asks them questions such as 'How many instruments do you hear?' and 'Stand when you hear the cymbal.' (This activity can include movement or the children adding their own percussive accompaniments.)
Tuesday	Reading	The class can perform choral reading of the words to the song (written on the chalkboard). After the first reading, delete one word from each line. After second reading, delete another word from each line. Continue if apropriate, or use it as a word substitution game.
Wednesday	Speaking	The children recite the words to the song. They could also recite using substitutions for rhyming words.
Thursday	Writing	The teacher writes selected alternate versions on chalkboard. The children have the chance to write their own if they wish.
Friday	Singing	The children can sing new versions of a well-known song, e.g. 'Baa baa black sheep' can become 'Moo moo jersey cow' or 'Quack quack yellow duck'.

Example 4 — Focus: Humorous poetry

Monday	Listening	Children listen to the teacher reading a selection of poems. (Note: if children have not learned to appreciate poetry, don't 'announce' that you are going to read poems — just read them! There are plenty that the children will ask for again and again. Some are listed below.)
Tuesday	Speaking	Children recite poems they know. (Children enjoy choral reading of poems they know. One way to teach them poems is to follow the procedure explained in the 'music' example above.)
Wednesday	Reading	Children read self-selected poems. (The teacher should collect as many poetry books as possible. Poems can be copied on to single sheets.)
Thursday	Writing	As a class, look at the different forms of poetry and discuss differences in the way they are written.
Friday	Writing	The whole class or groups try writing one form of poetry e.g. haiku, limerick, etc. (See relevant titles listed in Further Reading at the end of this chapter.)

In conclusion, and at the risk of being repetitious, please remember that these sessions are *not* intended to motivate children to write. The intention is to **expose** children to various forms of, and purposes for, writing.

Criteria for selecting activities

Below is a set of possible criteria for selecting curriculum activities. This list is not prescriptive and schools should adapt it, select from it, or reject it as they see fit.

All other things being equal, one activity is more worthwhile than another if it:

1　permits children to make informed choices in carrying out the activity and to reflect on the consequences of their choices;

2　assigns to children active roles in the learning situation rather than passive ones;

3　asks children to engage in inquiry into ideas, applications of intellectual processes, or current problems, either personal or social;

4　involves children with reality (i.e. real objects, materials, and artefacts);

5　can be completed successfully by children at several different levels of ability;

6　asks children to examine in a new setting an idea, an application of an intellectual process, or a current problem which has been previously studied;

7　requires children to examine topics or issues that citizens in our society do not normally examine — and that are typically ignored by the major communication media in the nation;

8　involves children and teachers in 'risk' taking — not a risk of life or limb, but a risk of success or failure;

9　requires children to rewrite, rehearse, and polish their initial efforts;

10　involves children in the application and mastery of meaningful rules, standards, or disciplines;

11　gives children a chance to share the planning, the carrying out of a plan, or the results of an activity with others;

12　is relevant to the expressed purposes of the children.[9]

---

9. Cited in Primary School Curriculum, Victorian Education Department, 1979, p.57. Adapted from Raths, James D., 'Teaching without Specific Objectives', *Educational Leadership*, April 1971, pp.714-20

Drafting — Revision

Pre-writing (Rehearsal, Incubation)

Writing

D CONTENT
- Listening to the text first of all for what the writer has to say.

R DETAIL AND SEQUENCE
- Asking the writer questions which stem from what is actually stated.

A
- Framing questions to help the writer become aware of important points or detail.

F
- Attending to vocabulary and sentence structure.

T
- Being specific with descriptive or evaluative comments.

I MECHANICS — CONVENTIONS
- Concentration on developing one skill at a time in relation to the use of conventional punctuation and grammar.

N
- Teaching at the point of need.

G
- Polishing handwriting and spelling.
- Helping writers to make their best better.

Publishing

Revision and drafting go hand in hand in the writing process. It is simpler to understand what is involved in the processes if we re-name revision, as Graves does, as 're-seeing'. Once children have been allowed to 're-see' their written work, the drafting process begins. Children alter their pieces as they see necessary in order to make the messages clearer, stronger and more readable. In some instances the writers do not really have a particular focus when they begin to write — therefore the revision is an integral part of drafting for meaning.

Revision, as seen in the drafting process, will illustrate the children's development as writers. Early writers may not revise at all. Getting an initial message down on paper fulfils their need completely. As their sense of purpose and audience develops, the need to revise and re-see to convey their message in the 'best' way becomes meaningful. As the writers' powers of revision evolve, they develop individual styles of drafting. This is to be encouraged and allows the teacher to assess each writer's understanding of the malleability of a written piece.

Once the revisions have developed from being purely 'cosmetic' (straightening up a letter, etc.), each writer will probably begin adding information, at first only to the end of a story, then to the beginning, and eventually within the body of the piece. Gradually, writers will develop methods of editing, re-sequencing and improving their piece, rather than copying out and making minor changes from draft to draft. We have observed children using various types of editing techniques including cutting and pasting (to re-organize), and stars, arrows and invented symbols to add information. Allow children to share and experiment with these ideas as 'the longest way round is *not always* the sweetest way home'. Let them discover short cuts.

How can we help children learn to draft?

There is no set formula, nor are there sequential steps that all children will follow in the drafting process. Because drafting involves revising or re-seeing by each individual writer, there cannot be a 'recipe' which is applicable to all writers.

What we can do is help children develop the skills of revision by learning to focus on *one* aspect or area at a time. These skills are developed and nurtured largely through questions asked of the writer during conference. These questions must always relate to the clarification of meaning. The writer is then able to ask him or herself — 'Have I said what I mean? Can I make it better? What might I do next?'

It is important that the teacher realizes that the types of questions and the direction of focus will change, depending on the working draft of the child.

Content
In early drafts of a piece, the focus should be on content. The teacher must close his or her eyes to spelling, grammar and mechanics and home in on questions which allow the child to make logical choices about what needs to be included or omitted, so that the information is clarified.

Detail/sequence
Once content is complete the next focal point is detail. The why's and when's and who's must be answered, e.g. 'Is your information in the correct order? Have you used the best possible words to express your thoughts?'.

This is the time for the writer to ensure his or her intentions are being successfully realized within the written work.

Mechanics-conventions
Because mechanics are only necessary for presentation to an audience, it is the last stage of drafting. The child looks at such things as handwriting and punctuation, which is always regarded as a means to clarify meaning for the reader, and then spelling. Usually the teacher and writer concentrate on one major teaching point at a time. The child may not be able to use a number of conventions (i.e. !, ? and " ") but the teacher should only choose one as a teaching point for this particular piece of work.

The teacher's role during drafting
The children need to see themselves as being able to choose direction and make decisions about the development of their drafts. They need to be able to see their writing as malleable. Graves likens the writing to clay. It can be modelled and re-modelled until it is just right. It is the teacher's role to help the child realize this by:

1 writing with the class. Let them see your methods of revising and changing things. Let them see writing can be difficult and messy, but also satisfying.
2 encouraging children to assume full responsibility for their writing. Let them make the decisions regarding length, format, content and focus.
3 acknowledging and encouraging individual differences in style and methods of working and editing. Provide silent and communal areas within the room. (What kind of writer are you? — See pre-writing.)

Revision stages	Suggestions for the next step
1 Children don't independently re-read or reconsider either their words or their mechanics. Writing is final, and for these children, it is extremely hard to put anything on paper at all.	These children can revise in other media. They should also be encouraged to re-read what they write. Questions like 'What is your favourite part?' help them begin to look back.
2 Some children re-read and correct their papers. They only make small changes, and they erase rather than cross out. They see each draft as a final copy.	By listening carefully to what this child writes and asking honest, real questions, the writer can learn that his or her reader needs more information. Content revision begins as 'adding-on'. Usually children first add on to the end of their piece, later they add to the middle sections.
3 Some children independently recopy their pieces. This is a step ahead of the child who merely corrects the original paper. Once there are two drafts, handwriting and spelling can be relegated to a later stage in the process, and the child can worry about content and language only. Also, as the child recopies he or she often changes the original.	The next step is to learn to make the first draft into a working manuscript; write all over it, annotate it, change it, use it.
4 Instead of viewing the second draft as a copy, the child begins to see it as a second try. Usually the child will at first disregard the first draft and do the second one 'from scratch'.	Encourage the child to use the first draft and ask questions such as: 'What did you learn from it?' 'What needs to be cut, saved or changed?' Look first to the larger issues (content, sequence, focus). Later look at language, word choice and precision.

4 allowing for variations in mood and inspiration. Ensure that there are adequate activities for children to carry on with if they 'run dry'.

Revision stages

There are several stages in the revision process that each child will work through. See page 18.[10]

The Writing Conference

The conference is the focal point of the writing process. It is the means by which the child discovers, clarifies, and refines what he or she wants to express. It is also the means through which the child comes to grips with the actual process being used and learns his or her areas of strength and weakness.

There are various types of conferences, each serving a different purpose and requiring varied responses. They include:

1 individual conference
2 group conference
3 small teaching groups (special issues conference or clinic)
4 publishing conference.

1 The individual conference

The individual conference, as implied by the name, is an interaction between one child and the teacher. It is only a short interaction to clarify a small problem that may be frustrating or hindering the development of the current draft. Questions that may arise are: 'What's the piece about?' 'What part of the piece is most important to you?'

These conferences mainly refer to focus and general content problems. They are brief and to the point, lasting no more than two to five minutes.

2 The group conference

The group conference usually involves up to five or six children who, with the aid of the teacher, discuss the focus, content, direction and expression of completed drafts. They should also look at things like the strong points of the piece and ways of building on them if necessary, and locating the weaker points of the piece and ways of strengthening them.

The effect of a conference on the children is the development of positive attitudes to ideas and criticism and confident relationships with others. Its value is to develop an audience awareness in each child through feedback from his or her group.

A conference provides an opportunity for total language — reading, listening, speaking, and writing — to be used in an integrated fashion.

> Children who experience a growing vocabulary in a natural setting of listening, talking, writing, and reading, move with ease to language that reflects desire, anticipation, evaluation, feelings, and hopes.'[11]

At all times the teacher must remember that the children should do most of the talking. It is the teacher's job to formulate questions that will help the children express themselves. Graves breaks the types of questions into three main groups.[12]

(a) Opening questions:
• What's the piece about?
• Why are you writing about it?
• How did you get started?
• What's your favourite part?

(b) Following questions:
These questions are often not really questions. They are often re-statements. 'You said that you were scared . . .'. The re-statements are designed to encourage the child to give more information about his or her topic.

---

10. For elaboration on revision stages see Calkins, Lucy, 'Make It Messy to Make It Clear', Educational Document 1978, University of New Hampshire, Morrill Hall Durham, N.H. 03824

11. Allen, Roach Van, *Language Experiences in Communication*, Houghton Mifflin Co., 1976, p.255

12. Graves, D., *Writing: Teachers and Children at Work*, Heinemann Educational Books, 1983

Sequence of activities	Language areas used	
	Writer	Audience
A child reads out the draft or part thereof.	reading ⟶	critical listening
The group responds to the writer by making comments, asking questions, or discussing the writing.	listening ⟵	speaking ↕ listening
The writer responds by answering questions or noting down comments which may assist when re-writing the piece.	speaking writing (note-taking) ⟶	listening
Using information drawn from the audience's responses, the child then rewrites or revises the drafts.	writing	

(c) Process questions:

These are the questions that lead the child to talk about what he or she has done (the process worked through) and to think about new avenues to take in developing the piece. Suggested questions are:

• What do you think you'll do next?
• I notice you changed your lead sentence. Why did you do that?
• How do you feel about your story?
• Are you happy with your beginning and ending?
• Explain how your title fits your story.
• What do you need help on?
• What questions did your conference partner have for you?
• Did you tell about something or did you show us by using examples?
• Can you think of a different way to say this?
• Does the beginning of your piece grab the reader's attention?
• What questions do you have of me?

Once children are familiar with conference questions and are able to predict the process which is ahead of them, 'self-conferencing' can become an integral part of the drafting process. The above questions can be classified into content, sequence and detail categories. These categories may be used as a focus for small teaching groups in helping children come to terms with the drafting process.

Response to children's writing

Teachers and children respond to different aspects of a child's written piece. Their response may be to the content and/or form.

The table at the top of page 21 shows some examples of the kind of responses that might be made and the aspects that they are referring to.

A group conference in action (lower primary)

Group conferences with early writers differ in that they occur *while* the writing is taking place.

The teacher sits with a group and writes his or her own 'story'. The teacher's topic has to be real — don't attempt set sentence patterns or oversimplified vocabulary! Teacher-modelling at this stage is vitally important. It helps children:

(a) with topic choice ('If the teacher writes about what happened last night, I can too!' etc.);

(b) learn conventions (children observe the teacher writing from left to right across the page, etc.);

(c) see the link between writing and other expressive arts (e.g. drawing is a legitimate part of what I want to put down on paper and helps me say what I want to say);

(d) extend their content (the teacher talks about his/her writing and makes comments such as 'I think it's important to put

Evaluation of content	'Good idea. Sounds like an interesting topic.'
Evaluation of structure	'I liked when you wrote . . .'
Encouragement	'This was very exciting. Tell me more about the part when . . .'
Attitude **Audience**	'Is this your best?'
Clarification of content **of form**	'I don't understand what happened here. Can you explain?' 'Which is your opening sentence?'
Elaboration of content **of form**	'What would this feel like?' 'Could you expand the second paragraph?'
Reaction to content **to form**	'I enjoyed that. I think that should be published.' 'I like the words you've chosen.'
Taking action	Have a small teaching group on quotation marks after seeing that a group is ready for it.
Moving outside writing (extension)	'Tell me more! Have you considered what the conference people suggested?'
Addition	'Have other people had that experience?'
General impression	'This story follows on well from your last written piece.'

this in because . . .' and 'Do you think I need this part in?' etc.);

(e) become aware of wide audiences (Is there enough information for someone who hasn't shared the experience?);

(f) learn terminology (children learn the 'language about language').

At the initial learning stage, drawing is usually an integral part of the story, so the teacher should also use drawing to help express meanings.

While the teacher is very much a part of the writing group, he or she needs to observe and attend to:

(a) writing behaviour;
(b) interaction of individuals within the group;
(c) the willingness of individuals to take risks;
(d) a child's attention to message through drawing/writing;
(e) a child's willingness to use references (e.g. other people, word chart, alphabets, books, etc.);

(f) each child's directional habits (in addition to the conventions, this will also include use of space, layout, etc.);

(g) each child's handwriting (letter formation, willingness to use a range of different writing implements);

(h) each child's attempts to spell (see chapter 6 on spelling).

It should now be evident that conferences and small teaching groups run back to back at the initial writing stage. Issues which would be dealt with separately beyond this first stage are dealt with 'in the one sitting'. However, even with early writers it is essential for the teacher to attend to the message or content *first*. Handwriting skills, spelling attempts and so on, are attended to after meanings have been shared and discussed. Also, the teaching points which need to be made are most often handled on a one-to-one basis.

Note: Revision (in the sense of re-drafting or re-writing) is not common with early writers.

What is important to the writer today may be forgotten tomorrow when a completely new 'story' will be attempted. It should be seen as great progress when writers choose to continue with the work of the previous day.

A group conference in action (middle and upper primary)

Usually the children sit around in a comfortable setting. (Up to five children and a teacher is suggested).

One child reads out the current draft or part thereof. She or he would begin by stating the draft number ('This is my third draft . . .') and then the title of the piece. He or she might then read the whole piece while the group listens, but most often, the writer will only read the part which requires feedback.

When the reading is finished, the group receives the piece ('That was great!', 'I liked the part where . . .') and then often asks for more information ('Tell me more about . . .', 'What did you mean by . . .?'). The group would then make comments on the writing which usually focus on the writer's purpose, content, or style.

The type of response that the group makes to a piece of writing in a conference situation is usually determined by the stage (draft number) the piece of writing has reached. In the early drafts the responses/comments should concentrate more on the **content**, but as a piece nears publication, its **form** (particularly style, punctuation, and grammar) becomes more important.

3 Small teaching groups

Otherwise known as special issues conferences or clinic groups, these deal with specific mechanical problems, i.e. punctuation, grammar, word usage etc. The need for small teaching groups becomes evident during conference. The teacher must be alert to errors or problems that individuals are having, but rather than interrupt a conference which is primarily dealing with content, they should simply note down the problem. On the following day the teacher can set aside time to teach the necessary skills needed for the current piece of writing. Teaching at the point of need is suc-

cessful and satisfying (see the next section on small-teaching groups for more information).

4 Publishing conferences

These are almost totally child-based and are used mainly in the upper school. The children review published stories with the aim of selecting one for wider audience publication. Stories are selected by consensus opinion on the basis of suitability in book form, originality of subject area, and evidence of personal effort by the author.

The important thing to remember when evaluating your conferences is that if you (the teacher) have done most of the talking, your conference has failed. The hardest thing for the teacher to do is to let the children arrive at their opinions and decisions themselves.

Conference reminders:
(a) Listen to the child.
(b) Respond to content first — leave conventions to last!
(c) A teacher's job is to follow, not lead. Allow the writing task to remain with the *child*.
(d) Handle one problem at a time.
(e) Keep it short.

The writing process

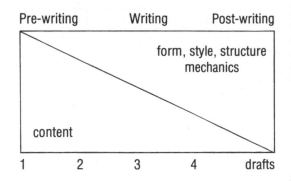

This diagram illustrates how the emphasis in writing changes over a succession of drafts.[13]

---

13. Succession of Drafts, adapted from Murray, D., 'How Writing Finds Its Own Meaning', *Theory Into Practice*, Teaching Composition, N.C.T.E., 1980

The Teacher's Role in Conference

The teacher interacts with the child for ideas, but is deliberately not involved with the drawing or planning of the writing. However the teacher does try to establish more information by asking deliberate questions which extend, support, and nurture the writer's process. He or she should always listen, consult and ask, rather than tell.

The teacher should emphasize not only what the writer knows about the topic, but also the fact that the writer is in control of the writing. He or she is involved in a process of leading the children to help themselves as individuals or as a group to:

(a) learn conventions;
(b) appreciate feelings;
(c) notice similarities;
(d) develop ideas;
(e) react to an audience;
(f) seek information;
(g) receive the writing of others;
(h) ask relevant questions.

Teachers develop their own styles of conferencing. They generally adapt the conference to meet each child's need of the moment. The model that they project is very important in encouraging all children within the group to respond and contribute to discussion.

Small Teaching Groups (Clinic Groups)

Young writers need time to run into their own problems, to ask their own questions. Only then can skills be learned in context — for the context is not the subject matter, but the child's question, the child's need.[14]

When children write regularly, they are able to give greater attention to their information, and they reflect on the craft of writing itself. The 'mechanics' (handwriting, spelling and punctuation) and the grammar which children need to know at primary school, can be taught and learned through conferences called small teaching groups, which are conducted when the child's needs arise, not at inappropriate and irrelevant times as whole class exercises. They are usually conducted with only small groups of children working with a teacher, however, occasionally issues will be relevant for larger groups.

Small teaching groups usually focus on the development of a particular skill and normally

---

14. Calkins, L., 'When Children Want to Punctuate' in Walshe, R. D. (ed.), *Donald Graves in Australia*, P.E.T.A., 1981, p.90

last for only one writing session, but this may vary according to the needs of the group.

The children usually decide themselves when they want a small teaching group on a particular topic or skill. Teachers will sometimes decide to hold one on a skill which needs to be developed at a certain time. For example, there may be several children who have demonstrated in their work that they are ready for further work on using paragraphs, so the teacher would prepare a small teaching group lesson on this area.

The basis of the small teaching group is the children's own writing. The discussion centres around each individual's drafts and the progress or problems he or she is having. The children should leave a small teaching group with a particular task or skill to apply to their own writing.

Opportunity for sharing what happened in the group is usually provided at the end of each language session.

Some areas to consider during small teaching groups

1 **Editing** — Discuss and share ways of marking corrections when proof-reading.

2 **Punctuation** — Show the children how to use paragraphs, commas, quotation marks, exclamation marks, capital letters, etc.

3 **Spelling approach** — Discuss approaches to spelling. Use 'Have-a-go' cards (see p. 61), dictionaries, class lists, spelling strategies ('look-cover-write-check method'). Proof-read for spelling errors. Children can make personal lists of words they have trouble spelling.

4 **Revision** — Discuss: how to add new information; how to delete information; how to re-arrange words, sentences and paragraphs to allow a more logical order; how to draft; how to choose a better word. Demonstrate aids to revision: cut and paste; arrows; leaving space to allow extra information to be added; etc.

5 **How to choose a topic** — Discuss interests and experiences. Brainstorm. Share topics completed by others in the grade.

6 **How to choose a title** — Talk about the importance of catching and keeping the interest of an audience and how a title needs to be catchy. List possible titles; choose the best. Look at titles of books and headlines in newspapers.

7 **Awareness of audience** — Discuss communication. Who is the intended audience? Has the writing been aimed at them? Is the writing clear and correct?

8 **How to use resources to aid writing** — Talk to children about the importance of

listing, note-taking, recording, and organizing information. Show them how to use a dictionary, the library, keep word lists, interview people etc.

9 **How to plan a piece of writing** — Go through the steps necessary to plan a piece of writing: brainstorming, 'ideas page', collecting information, imagining, exploring, researching, selecting, sequencing. Rehearse in different media (drama, drawing, dance, modelling).

10 **Publishing** — Explore different ways of publishing and all the associated facets (design, layout, illustrations, photography, bookbinding, display etc.).

Publication

The most important influence on any writer is the audience — that is, when there is a prospect of 'publication'. Children need this stimulus too; otherwise they are being asked to write for exercise purposes only — which means, for a communication non-event.

Given an audience through publication, children can be shown that real writing begins only after the first draft has been written: in the polishing and redrafting that at length produces writing fit for publication.[15]

What is publishing?

Publishing means 'to make public'. Consequently, publishing may take many forms varying from simple oral reading to sophisticated productions requiring a team of people.

Early writers may simply read out their writing to the teacher, a group of children, or even a friend. This writing has now become public in a very real sense. With these early writers, publication follows immediately after the first draft.

Alternatively, publication may mean showing or displaying the work. It could be pinned up for a day or held up for discussion. Since the spelling at this stage may not be conventionally

correct, it would be inappropriate to have this work on long-term display. In fact, having the work displayed just on the day it is written will be enough, as children at this stage will often write about a new topic the next day. The point we wish to make is that if work is going to be published in print with the intention of that writing becoming **reading** material, it should be in the correct form.

With writers who are re-drafting or revising their work, there is a need to 'make your best better' as a pre-requisite for publication. In the process of revision, children become responsible for corrections. A piece ready for publication must contain the courtesies of correct spelling, punctuation, grammar and good handwriting for its readers. In a pre-publishing conference or a conference on final drafts, the focus is on editing and proof-reading. (For example, the teacher should ask questions such as 'How have you checked spelling?', 'Are there any words which should be taken out?', 'How have you shown that there are people talking?' etc.)

Another point that needs to be stressed is that at the publication stage, the writing is not 'taken away' from the writer. Final decisions about content, title, and so on, must be made by the *author* who must also attend to conventions (the typist should not be left to decipher rough drafts).

When involved in group publication, the author should remain in control of publishing decisions about illustrations, layout, form of publication, etc. It is important that the writer is involved in these decisions for it is here that teachers will attend to the 'Things I Can Do' list inside the back cover of the writing folder (see p. 40). Attention will be given to two aspects:

1 Skills already listed under 'Things I Can Do' will be checked to see if they have been used in the written piece, e.g. if a child has previously shown she or he can competently or independently use quotation marks but has failed to do so in the current piece, then the responsibility for their insertion is with the writer.

2 New skills demonstrated will be added to the list. Only those things demonstrated in the

---

15. P. Edwards, '100 Ways to Publish Children's Writing', cited in Walshe, R. D. (ed.), *Better Reading/Writing — Now!*, P.E.T.A., 1980

writing *and* articulated are listed. It is through the 'pre-publishing' conference that the child articulates his or her understandings. The ability to articulate the understanding does not mean that the child has to know and use sophisticated linguistic terminology! It is sufficient evidence that a child understands the proper use of exclamation marks when the child says 'I put it there because I wanted you to know that the person was shouting.' It is not necessary for the child to say, 'I used an exclamation mark there because exclamation marks are used to express some strong feeling such as surprise, wonder or appreciation.' (Note: The second definition comes from a Primary English text!)

The author may expect assistance from the 'publishing committee' (with conventions, layout, illustrations, etc.) but he or she *must* be involved in this 'polishing'.

Some publishing ideas

1 Ideas for displaying day-to-day work

(a) Display

 i sentences and phrases to begin stories. Draw from examples of children's opening sentences and published work.

 ii quotes taken from children's writing on a 'famous quotes' board.

 iii headlines from newspapers (use these as an introduction to talking about the children's story titles).

(b) Set up an attractive and comfortable setting for conferences to take place. Perhaps include a display of finished books or published pieces of writing.

(c) Use an old picture frame to display their photograph with their writing. Write on a card under the photograph 'Writers of the Week' or 'Introducing Our Grade'.

(d) On a large board, stick sheets of coloured paper to form a large patchwork quilt. Each pupil selects a 'patch' and undertakes to fill it with well-decorated, polished writing of any kind. Don't rush the writing. Make this a slowly emerging project which yields something that children are proud of.

(e) Make a 'mail train' with each carriage containing a story, paragraph or poem.

(f) Cut out some brightly coloured balloon and kite shapes and paste on to or write on them poems or short stories.

2 Publish books of all kinds

(a) A collection of stories written by the class about personal experiences, entitled 'Things you didn't know about us'.
(b) Riddle and joke books
(c) 'What do you know about' books, e.g. 'What do you know about sharks?'
(d) 'How to' books, e.g. 'How to make spaghetti'
(e) Poetry collections
(f) Individual stories
(g) Group stories
(h) Stories written by the teacher
(i) Stories written by parents
(j) Recipe books

3 Write letters

Encourage children to write letters or notes to other children, teachers, parents, other schools, their favourite authors, aunts and uncles etc.

4 Hold special displays and exhibitions

Consider shop and/or library displays of the children's writing. Submit work to the local newspaper.

5 Make/discuss:

(a) story mobiles
(b) posters
(c) cards — birthday, thank you, congratulations, special events, festivities (Easter, Christmas etc.) and seasons
(d) murals

A guide to group publishing

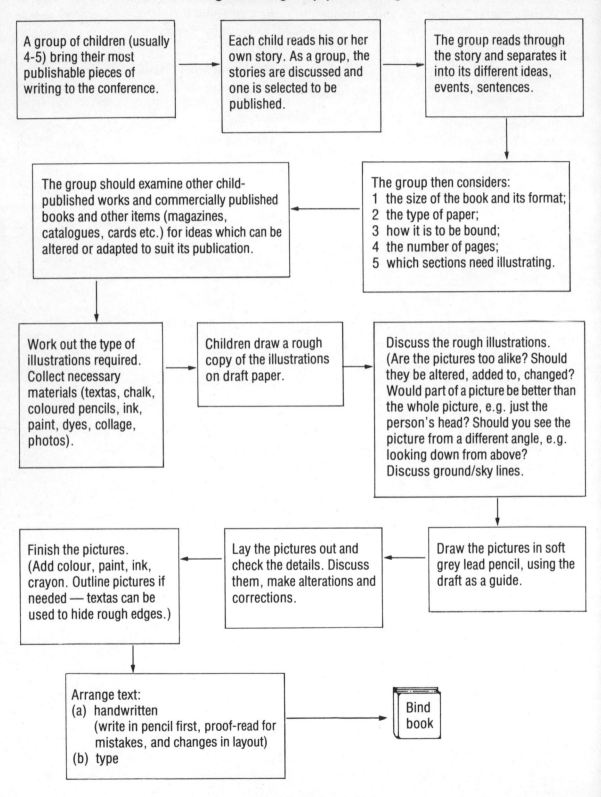

A group of children (usually 4-5) bring their most publishable pieces of writing to the conference.

→

Each child reads his or her own story. As a group, the stories are discussed and one is selected to be published.

→

The group reads through the story and separates it into its different ideas, events, sentences.

The group should examine other child-published works and commercially published books and other items (magazines, catalogues, cards etc.) for ideas which can be altered or adapted to suit its publication.

←

The group then considers:
1 the size of the book and its format;
2 the type of paper;
3 how it is to be bound;
4 the number of pages;
5 which sections need illustrating.

Work out the type of illustrations required. Collect necessary materials (textas, chalk, coloured pencils, ink, paint, dyes, collage, photos).

→

Children draw a rough copy of the illustrations on draft paper.

→

Discuss the rough illustrations. (Are the pictures too alike? Should they be altered, added to, changed? Would part of a picture be better than the whole picture, e.g. just the person's head? Should you see the picture from a different angle, e.g. looking down from above? Discuss ground/sky lines.

Finish the pictures. (Add colour, paint, ink, crayon. Outline pictures if needed — textas can be used to hide rough edges.)

←

Lay the pictures out and check the details. Discuss them, make alterations and corrections.

←

Draw the pictures in soft grey lead pencil, using the draft as a guide.

Arrange text:
(a) handwritten
      (write in pencil first, proof-read for
      mistakes, and changes in layout)
(b) type

→

Bind book

Further Reading

Introductory pre-writing activities

Allen, R. & Allen, C., *Language Experience Activities*, Houghton Mifflin and Co., Boston, 1976.

Hathorn, L., *Good To Read*, Methuen Aust. Pty Ltd, 1983.

Long, J., *Sparks: Language Arts Ideas for the Primary School*, Primary Education, Melbourne, 1978.

Rose, J., *Ignition: Language Arts Ideas for the Primary School*, Primary Education, Melbourne, 1981.

Schoenheimer, H. & Winch, G., *Living Language Series* ('I Can Touch the Sky', 'My World Is Everywhere', 'Silver in the Sunlight', 'Everything Dances, Everything Sings') Jacaranda, 1975.

Way, B., *Development through Drama*, Longman, London, 1973.

Poetry Books

Cole, William (Ed.), *Oh, what nonsense!* Methuen, 1968.
——. *Oh, how silly!* Methuen, 1971.
——. *Oh, that's ridiculous!* Methuen, 1972.
——. *Beastly boys and ghastly girls*. Methuen, 1970.

Dahl, R., *Revolting Rhymes*, Puffin, 1984.

Factor, J. (Compiler), *Far Out Brussel Sprout!*, O.U.P., 1983.

Fatchen, Max, *Songs for My Dog and Other People*, Kestrel/Puffin, 1983.

——., *Wry Rhymes for Troublesome Times*, Kestrel/Puffin, 1985.

McVitty, W. (Ed.), *Word Magic — Poetry as a Shared Adventure*, P.E.T.A., 1985.

Drafting (revision)

Calkins, L., 'What Children Show Us about Revision', in Walshe, R. (Ed.), *Donald Graves in Australia*, P.E.T.A., 1981.

Graves, D., 'Andrew Learns to Make Writing Hard', *Language Arts*, 56, 5, 1979.

Graves, D., 'Patterns of Child Control of the Writing Process', in Walshe, R. (Ed.), *Donald Graves in Australia*, P.E.T.A., 1981.

Petrosky, A. & Brozick, J., 'A Model for Teaching Writing Based Upon Current Knowledge of the Writing Process', *English Journal*, January, 1979.

Sowers, S., 'A Six-Year-Old's Writing Process — the First Half of First Grade', *Language Arts*, 57, 7, 1979.

The writing conference

Calkins, L., *Lessons from a Child*, Heinemann, 1983.

Graves, D., 'Balance the Basics: Let Them Write', *Learning*, 6, 8, April 1978.

Graves, D., *Writing: Teachers and Children at Work*, Heinemann, 1983.

Hill, K., *The Writing Process — One Writing Classroom*, Nelson, 1984.

Searle, D. & Dillon, D., 'Responding to Student Writing: What is Said or How it is Said', *Language Arts*, 57, 7, 1980.

Small teaching groups

Calkins, L., 'When Children Want to Punctuate' in Walshe, R. D. (Ed.), *Donald Graves in Aust*, P.E.T.A., 1981, pp. 89-96.

Walshe, R. D. (Ed.), *Every Child Can Write*, P.E.T.A., 1981.

Calkins, L., *Lessons from a Child*, Heinemann, 1983.

Graves, D., *Writing: Teachers and Children at Work*, Heinemann, 1983, pp. 151-205.

Publishing

Hill, K., *The Writing Process — One Writing Classroom*, Nelson, 1984.

Kohl, H., *Maths, Writing and Games in the Open Classroom*, Random House, 1974.

Pigdon, K. & Woolley, M., 'Decisions, Decisions', *The Educational Magazine*, 40, 2, 1983.

Walshe, R. D. (Ed.), *Better Reading/Writing — Now!*, P.E.T.A., 1977.

3 THE ROLE OF THE TEACHER

From the first day of school we must leave control of the writing with the child: the choice of topic and the writing itself.[1]

Perhaps one of the most important things to consider in a writing classroom is the shift of responsibility from the teacher to the child. No longer can the teacher be seen as the only authority, deciding the best direction for the child to follow. Rather, the teacher must become a 'tour guide', who can suggest avenues to take, the final decision must rest with the author.

'Children must be free to explore and make their own discoveries . . .'.[2] When your suggestions have been rejected, breathe a sigh of relief as your authors are showing confidence in their own abilities and have their own purposes to pursue. The most difficult part is getting started. Writing with the children is one of the most effective ways to begin. The teacher is a prominent example. Initially, the teacher should assess her or his own habits and attitudes to writing. A teacher who writes can serve as a model for the class as children very rarely see adults in the act of writing. 'There are many reasons why teachers must write. Writing regularly, they never forget that writing is difficult — for adults as well as children'.[3]

This activity also paves the way for the children to begin seeing the teacher as a real person who is willing to share. In turn, it encourages them to open up as people, not simply as students. It is of utmost importance that the children realize they are thought of as functioning people, with interests and areas of expertise inside and outside the classroom walls. We must help them realize their own self-worth if we are to expect them to 'bare their souls' in the writing process. Teaching writing is teaching a craft. The writing teacher must practice writing alongside the children.

1. Graves, D., 'Children Want to Write', cited in Walshe, R. D. (ed.), *Donald Graves in Australia*, P.E.T.A., 1981
2. DeFord, D., 'Literacy: Reading Writing and Other Essentials, *Language Arts*, 58, 6, 1981
3. Graves in Walshe, op. cit., p.8

One of the main objectives of the writing teacher is to help the children see they have something to say that is of interest to others and that the written word is one of the best ways of reaching a wide audience. This is no easy task in the initial stages of the writing program. There are no quick solutions. Once the children have 'opened up', the teacher should ensure that they begin using others as resources for their own writing. The teacher needs to recognize the children as being informed people and help them utilize areas of expertise among their peers. 'Often not anxious to ask for teacher assistance, students can turn to each other for help.'[4]

The writing teacher must be prepared to spend time talking and listening to children, getting to really know each individual and helping them realize that they have something of worth to offer. Everyone does if you dig deep enough! The teacher must *believe* that talk is *not* a waste of time, since talk establishes the initial foundations of acceptance.

The teacher is responsible for creating an environment where the child never feels threatened to discuss feelings, fears, strengths or abilities. The development of this sharing 'community' is paramount to the success of an effective writing classroom.

In summary, a writing teacher should:

- have a positive attitude to writing, understanding its nature and process.
- have an understanding of 'how' children learn.
- demonstrate the relevance of writing to life by exposing children to writers and various forms of writing, e.g. visiting the local newspaper office, excursions to the State library, inviting children's authors to talk to the class.
- demonstrate a range of forms and techniques for writing.
- introduce students to useful aids to writing — techniques for getting started, methods of revision.
- provide opportunities for writing each day in the classroom.

- encourage children to take risks and experiment with different styles and forms.
- create a supportive learning environment and allow time to produce a quality product.
- never imply greater knowledge of a topic.
- value children's choice of topic or form of writing.
- be an active member of the writing classroom.
- foster an honest relationship with writers. The children/teacher relationship should be built on sincerity and genuine interest.
- place children in a position of authority in relation to their audience.
- help writing to reach its intended audience.
- provide students with real experiences of authorship — class publications, newsboard etc. and extend the circulation of student writing beyond the classroom walls, i.e. newsletters etc.
- have definite expectations that each child will write something each day.

Further Reading

Calkins, L., 'Children Learn the Writer's Craft', in Walshe, R (ed.) *Donald Graves in Australia*, P.E.T.A., 1981.

Searle, D & Dillon, D., 'Responding to Student Writings — What is Said or How it is Said', *Language Arts*, 57, 7, October 1980.

Walshe, R. (ed.), *Better Reading/Writing — Now!*, P.E.T.A., 1977.

---

4. Klein, M., 'Teaching Writing in the Elementary Grades', *Elementary School Journal*, 81, 5, May 1981

4 ORGANIZATION

When considering the physical environment of the classroom there are several things to keep in mind.

1 Children will need special attention at special times.
2 Children will be working at differing paces.
3 Children will be needing different equipment at different times.
4 Not all children will always be working on a topic which enables them to write lucidly.

Let's take those four statements one at a time.

1 As a teacher, there will be constant demands on you to be either: conducting clinics, conducting group conferences, or conducting individual conferences.

These tasks inevitably require lots of time. In order to do them effectively, the teacher needs to be as free as possible from the more mundane tasks of distributing equipment, directing children in activities or organizing the class 'en masse'. It is important that from the outset the teacher helps the children learn the routine of the classroom as quickly as possible, to eliminate mundane interruptions.

2 Children will be working at different paces. Consequently some will be rehearsing, some will be drafting, revising, editing or publishing. Each of these stages need different working conditions — and some children prefer different types of working conditions.

Therefore it is helpful if the room is set up in two areas. One area can function as a group writing area in which children can talk and share as they write. Open tables grouped together work well, and the children should know that if they are working at one of those tables they can talk quietly.

The other area should be set aside as a quiet writing area for children who do not like to be interrupted while writing. One way of doing this is to staple corrugated cardboard around desks (similar to library corrals) where one or two children can work in solitude.

A conference area is also desirable. This should be a quiet comfortable area where a group of up to eight people can sit around to share and discuss their work. Bean-bags and cushions make this area cosy and some form of curtain to section it off helps to make it a special area.

3 Children will be needing different equipment at different times. It is of course desirable that the class does not need to call on the teacher to meet these needs. Some corner of the room could be set up as a writing centre to house all necessary items. It should contain:
(a) a variety of papers (e.g. blank, lined, large, coloured, card, etc.)
(b) scissors
(c) sticky-tape and glue
(d) a collection of writing utensils
(e) staplers and staples.
    Children should be free to go to this centre — but must also be responsible for keeping it tidy and well stocked.

4 Not all children will be working on a topic they can write about easily. These children must also be catered for (otherwise they will run amok and 'sabotage' the room). Activity centres (e.g. library, science, construction, games etc.) that the children can go to between topics or drafts could be set up. These centres can also contain interesting snippets from magazines that the children can add to. Time spent in these centres could well spark an idea for a new topic.

'My room's not big enough for all that' you may well say. Most classrooms already contain the above mentioned types of equipment; it's just that they are not always organized or easily accessible. Often equipment is stored in a cupboard and forgotten. Equipment is obviously put to better use when it is always available. For example, the science centre could well be one of the cupboards under the chalkboard. As long as it is accessible to children, it can function as an activity centre.

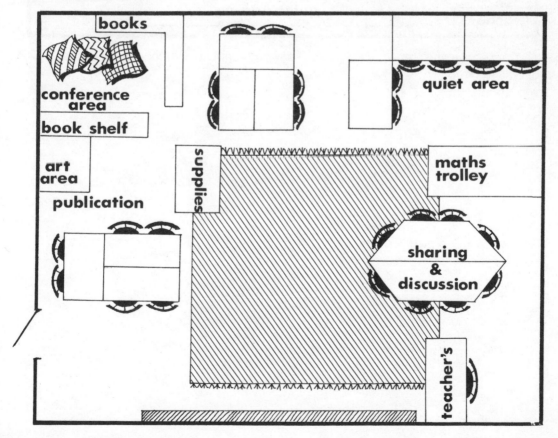

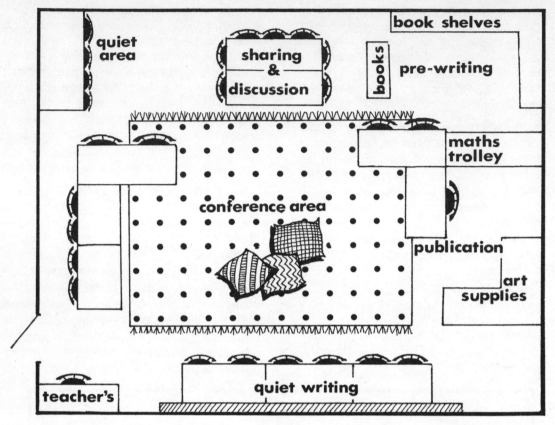

The diagram above and on the previous page show two suggested arrangements for the furniture in your classroom.

Daily Management Plans

Below are two suggested plans for a break-down of time in a writing session. The first is for lower primary children and the second for middle to upper primary children.

Note: Many teachers prefer to start the whole class writing. As children finish their 'pen to paper' work, they go immediately to one of the other activities.

15-20 minutes	**Weekly focus** — Introductory language activity which may include reading, speaking, listening, or writing, poetry, drama, singing, games.
35 minutes (Time varies with children's writing experience.)	**Writing time** — children continue writing drafts. Teacher writing may also occur here (see p.22 'A Conference in Action'). The teacher will have a conference with individuals or small groups while children are writing. Teaching of skills is usually individualized and related to a child's particular need (i.e. individual or small teaching groups are back to back with the conference. See p. 19). Individual activities may include word banks, shared sentences, quiet reading, word matching etc.
10-15 minutes	**Share time** — could include: 1 whole grade special issues conferences for common areas of concern 2 reading pieces aloud for a wider audience (oral publication) 3 discussion.

10 minutes	**Introductory language activity** — weekly focus 1 pre-writing 2 teacher writing
30-40 minutes	**Writing time** — the children continue writing drafts, rehearsing, discussing, conferencing, reading. The teacher may: 1 write with children 2 take a conference group 3 take a small-teaching group 4 move around the room working with individuals.
5-10 minutes	**Share time** — children share such things as: 1 excerpts from their writing 2 'quotes to quote' 3 their advances in process (e.g. new ways of drafting/revising discovered) 4 feedback from their small teaching groups 5 information from their folders 6 any newly-published book which can be read out 7 knowledge of their 'expert' areas.

Some teachers may be more comfortable running briefer workshop sessions while introducing a new routine.

If more time is available, then the writing time could be extended or further language activities could be included.

	½ class	½ class
15-20 mins	Introductory activity with the whole class. At the end of this session, small groups are directed to independent activities which may include:	
30 mins	**Writing time** Children begin/continue writing. Teacher may: 1 write with the children 2 take a conference group 3 take a clinic group 4 work with individuals. As the children finish, they move on to other language activities.	***Learning centres** — sand tray activities — science/nature activities — dress-up corner — shop corner — game centre etc. ***Task cards** — see P.E.N. 23 (a P.E.T.A. publication) — tasks cards attached to learning centres — handwriting tasks — bead threading cards — spelling activities etc. ***Wall story activities** ***Language experience activities**
10-15 mins	Share time with the whole class or small groups.	

* Many of these activities lead children into other forms of writing required for various purposes.

Above is an alternative daily management plan for teachers who prefer to divide their class into two groups. It is especially appropriate for lower year levels.

Further Reading

Boomer, G. (ed.), *Negotiating the Curriculum*, Ashton Scholastic, 1982.

Education Department of Victoria, *Primary School Curriculum: a Manual for Victorian Schools*, 1979.

Fleet, A & Martin, L., *Thinking It Through*, Nelson, 1984.

Holt, J., *What Do I Do Monday?*, Dell Publishing Co Inc., 1974.

Many of the Primary English Notes published by P.E.T.A. are useful.

5 RECORD-KEEPING AND EVALUATION

Processes involved in improving the writing program

1 Collecting and analysing data
2 Evaluation
3 Development

These three processes are on-going.

In order to evaluate and develop writing or any of its aspects, it is necessary to have appropriate information or data. This information should be:

1 relevant; and
2 organized and analysed.

Considerations[1]

1 Are we clear about the purposes for which we are gathering the data?
2 Do we know how the data will be used and in what form it can be most usefully presented?
3 What is the simplest and most straightforward way to get the information we want?
4 Will more complex data collection methods give us enough extra information to justify the additional time, trouble, and expense?
5 Have we got a range of different sorts of data to provide checks and balances on our information? (No one item or type of information can give us all the data we need to make valid evaluative judgements.)

Record-keeping

The following types of records we found useful for the evaluation of the children's work. They are:

1 weekly record
2 conference/small teaching group records
3 pupil writing folder
4 writing record
5 'Title Tally'
6 class collections
7 word banks/class lists

---

1. *The Primary School Curriculum: A Manual for Victorian Schools*, 1979, pp.96-97

Who Are the Records for?

	Teacher	Child	Parent	School
1 weekly record	✓			✓
2 conference/small teaching group records	✓			
3 writing folder	✓	✓	✓	✓
4 writing record	✓	✓		✓
5 'Title Tally'	✓	✓	✓	✓
6 class collections	✓	✓	✓	✓
7 word banks, class lists	✓	✓	✓	

1 Weekly record

General impressions and observations of workshop sessions, contact with individual children and/or small groups and children's behaviour are noted in the weekly program.

It can consist of the work program, record of procedure and a journal or diary.

The information recorded assists the teacher's evaluation of completed language activities and assists future planning particularly in relation to potential focus for the following week.

See the sample record on the opposite page.

2 Conference/small teaching group records

Through questions asked, the teacher is constantly assessing how each writer is progressing with their piece. Questions asked ultimately assist children to ask similar questions of themselves at different stages during the writing process. Thus conferences assist self-evaluation.

Conferences provide information about the child's progress with reference to:

1 how he or she is tackling or sorting out a topic;
2 his or her appreciation, response, participation and social development.

Points of interest or need may be recorded during the conference or small teaching groups on display cards. These may then be positioned around the room for future reference or revision. Since pupils are involved in the compilation of these charts, **it is important that the wording be**, **as far as possible**, **their own**. That is, that it makes sense to them.

Monday	**Children to Check**

INTRODUCTORY ACTIVITY/TEACHER WRITING
'Sounds Jubilee'
Interview teacher - trip to Malaysia, Thailand
CONFERENCE GROUP
Random individual conference
SMALL TEACHING GROUP
Whole grade - topic list check
SHARING TIME
Ishara - trip to Mildura / Swan Hill

Tuesday

INTRODUCTORY ACTIVITY/TEACHER WRITING
Interview - role play, Andrew as international
airline pilot
CONFERENCE GROUP
Kim, Lisa, Cindy, Robert
SMALL TEACHING GROUP
Samantha, Ishara, - publishing
SHARING TIME
Teacher; currency from Malaysia/Thailand.

Mark } check for
Jason } completed
pieces

Wednesday

INTRODUCTORY ACTIVITY/TEACHER WRITING
Brainstorming for new topic selection - holidays,
activities, likes/dislikes, etc.
CONFERENCE GROUP
Sue, Andrew - pre-publishing
SMALL TEACHING GROUP
Whole grade - vocab. lists for 'Holidays'
SHARING TIME
Sally - Knitting; Andrew - Book on Japan

Andrew)
Lisa } publishing
Cassie } group
Jason)

Thursday

INTRODUCTORY ACTIVITY/TEACHER WRITING
Vocab. lists - complete
Titles Tally - Commence Title Top Ten
CONFERENCE GROUP
Steven E., Lisa - first draft
SMALL TEACHING GROUP
Whole grade - self-questioning for comprehension of piece
SHARING TIME
Title Top Ten

Jamie - character
development

Friday

INTRODUCTORY ACTIVITY/TEACHER WRITING
Sharing topic selection
CONFERENCE GROUP
Shaun, Ekbal, Tim, Sam
SMALL TEACHING GROUP
Leigh, Cassie - getting focus for main idea
SHARING TIME
'Quotes to Quote' - on board

Shaun - final copy

3 Pupil writing folder

This is kept by the child and referred to by the child, teacher and parents. It contains three main sections:

(a) **Things I might write about**: The child lists possible writing topics. Not all of these will be written about.

   The teacher notes this section to see if the child needs assistance in choosing topics.

(b) **Things I can do/Things I know about**: The teacher completes a list of skills that the child has demonstrated in his or her writing.

   The child asks the teacher to check her or his drafts prior to publication ('pre-publishing'). The teacher looks through the drafts and notes down on the list any new skills not already listed. Each new skill is dated with its first appearance and the title of the draft it appeared in is also written down. The child checks through this list prior to publication as an aid to editing.

   Areas of interest may also be listed here. For example, a child may have listed on his or her folder such items as B.M.X. Bikes, Pigeons, Racing Cars, Knitting, Cartoon Drawing, that is, personal areas of 'expertise'.

(c) **Things I have written about**: The child lists topics which have been completed and the date they were published.

THINGS I HAVE WRITTEN ABOUT

TITLE	DATE COMPLETED
1. The day I split my head open	25·2·82
2. The day I baby-sat my cousin	23.3.82.
3. When we got our new swimming pool.	12.4.82
4. Curly	24.4.82
5. Swan Hill	9.8.82
6. Bobby Dazzler	20.10.82

My Writing Folder

Tania Brearly
Grade 6 Room 3

THINGS I CAN DO

Tania Knows: Grade 6

1. how to use capital letters for names of people ("Day I split My Head Open" Dr. 1)
2. how to use quotation marks.
3. how to use exclamation marks.
4. how to keep the correct tense.
5. how to revise by * adding information
   * cutting out unecessary info.
   * re-ordering information
6. how to use an apostrophe to s ownership/possession (Judy's
7. how to use an apostrophe f contractions (eg: didn't "
8. how to indent when beg piece or paragraph (Chrisie's Party 20/7/
9. the importance of a sentence to get th

Things I might write about:

1. When I split my head open ✓
2. The day I baby-sat my cousin ✓
3. When we got our new swimming pool ✓
4. Camp Swan Hill ✓
5. When we went to Cooma
6. When I went to Luna Park
7. Do you snore, Aliesha?
8. Judy's seance
9. Happy Birthday Tania
10. Bobby Dazzler ✓

Rebecca knows: Grade 2

1. how to name all the letters of the alphabet

2. how to use a capital letter to start a sentence.

3. how to use a fullstop to finish a sentence.

4. how to cross out and 'mess-up' her story to make it better.

5. how to use capital letters for a person's name.

6. how to change the order of her story to make it 'sensible'.

7. how to use 'talking marks' to show when someone talks (early Nov.)

Writing folder Grade 2

Craig knows: Grade 4

1. that from one large first draft, we can form different pieces (eg. from 'Lakes Entrance' → 'At Lakes Entrance,' 'Fishing'... Feb/March '82).

2. how to follow on <u>one</u> main idea in a draft and rewrite that idea to make it clear (eg. At Lakes Entrance Feb ;82).

3. that factual information can add interest to a piece (eg.'Fishing' – information about flatheads, bream, March '82).

4. that a catchy title is important to get a reader's attention (eg.'The Part That Makes Me Nervous,' July '82).

5. that the title of a piece may change between drafting and publishing (eg. 'School Sports' → 'The Part That Makes Me Nervous ').

6. that sentences begin with a capital.

7. that sentences end with a fullstop.

8. how to 'build up' excitement in a piece by giving interesting detail '... 400 metre mark and I was coming fourth. I was still in with a chance. 500 metre mark and I was coming third.' (Pre pub. 2/8/82).

9. how to use a word bank to correct spelling errors and 'have a go' at new words.

10. how to make changes to a piece in conference, to help improve the piece in re-drafting.

11. how to use a dictionary to help with spelling new words (August).

12. that good handwriting is important in a final copy for readers to understand.

13. that when we list things or people, we use a comma to take the place of 'and' (eg.'I was in that with Jamie, Michael and Jason', Sep. '82, 'The Part That Makes Me Nervous ').

Writing folder Grade 4

Susan knows: Grade 6

1	that sentences begin with a capital letter (Yabamac piece) Feb 9-17
2.	that proper nouns begin with a capital (Anna-Shelley Lodge) (Yabamac piece Feb.9-17)
3.	when redrafting, how to focus on a particular area to improve (Yabamac piece Feb.9-17)
4.	that commas may be used to break up a sentence "
5.	that using <u>adverbs</u> adds impact to a piece (eg. Anna and I walked <u>carelessly</u>).
6	that when writing a title in a piece, we use quotation marks (eg. "The Kangas")
7.	the difference between <u>their</u> and <u>there</u> (spelling and usage).
8.	how to join short sentences to form a more interesting sentence by using conjunctions (joining words).
9.	when writing direct conversation we use talking marks ("That lightning nearly hit us.")
10.	that a strong conclusion is important in "rounding off" a piece of writing (eg. "We were soon settled in and I drifted down into a deep sleep....").
11	the importance of numbering and dating drafts (Drafts 1-3 9/2/83 → 17/2/83.)
12.	that conversation is an interesting way to begin a piece of writing (Draft 1 "Fiddler on the Roof 9/3/83).
13.	that information in a draft may be revised by pasting over sections of the working draft ("Kitsy Drafts 1&2 10/3/83.).
14.	that conversation may be used in a piece to relate information in an interesting way ("Kitsy" Drafts 1-3 9/3 → 27/4/83).
15	how to use an apostrophe (') for contractions ("Kitsy" Draft 2. can't → can not we'll → we will).

Writing folder Grade 6

Susan knows:	Grade 6

16.	how to proof-read pre-publishing drafts for final corrections before publishing (Pre-pub. "Kitsy" 5/4/83)
17.	that many stronger words may be used in place of "said" (eg. asked with enthusiasm, answered, whispered ... Pre-pub "Kitsy" 5/4/83).
18.	that using detail and description in a piece holds the reader's interest ("Kitsy" May 83).
19	when writing questions, a question mark is used (Whereabouts? Yes? Pre-pub "Kitsy").
20.	how to lead a publishing group for book publication - be the editor pub conference group May '83.
21.	that by focusing on a group of objects and linking them together, a good mystery can be unfolded (Drafts 1-4 "Mystery of Silver Hairclip June-July83)
22.	how to draw up (draft) a plot for a fiction piece (Drafts 1-4).
23.	that a strong opening sentence is important to get a reader "hooked"
24.	how to "set the scene" and give background information through conversation at the beginning of a piece (Pre-pub "Silver Hairclip" 5/9/83).
25.	to make a word "stand out" and have emphasis, we can use capital letters (eg. "LOOK!" pre-pub "Silver Hairclip" 5/9/83).
26.	when we quote the name or title of something, we use quotation marks (eg. Pub "Pyap" - "I was on the 'Pyap' in Swan Hill" 22/7).
27.	how to use an apostrophe of posession to show ownership (eg. "I was in Miss Parry's group." Pub "Pyap" 22/7)
28.	we can give background information or detail by using brackets (eg. Sherrin and Gordon stood ... Sherrin (who manages Murray Downs lodges) and Gordon (our humorous bus driver) "Pyap" 22/7.

Identifying writing development

Skills listed under 'Things I Can Do' can be classified according to their place in the process development, viz:

Process development	What is demonstrated
Dating and numbering of drafts.	Classification and records of own progress. Indexation for later relocation.
Focus on main idea, e.g. deletion or expansion in drafts.	Ability to overview own content objectively as well as subjectively.
Sequencing, i.e. correct ordering of ideas.	Ordering information.
Detail, e.g. *best* way to convey an idea.	Choice of information.
Title selection — working title — published title.	May reflect change in focus *or* be more representative of main idea/focus.
STYLE/FORM — conversation — narrative — analogy — poetic — expository	Awareness of the variety of ways of expressing ideas through writing.
VOICE	Development and awareness of *own* tone in a piece of writing.
STRUCTURE	Opening sentence; body, main idea clarification; climax; conclusion.
Editing symbols, e.g. arrows, lining out, pasting over, cut and paste, etc. Referencing: Use of sources, e.g. peers, teacher, other writers, writing folder, charts, books, etc.	Refinement of revision skills. Development of purpose in proof-reading. Preparation for re-writing/publishing and adaptation of conference and reference ideas. Realization that often there is a need to draw on the knowledge and experience of others.
PUBLISHING — visual interpretation — individual or team production.	Awareness of a broader audience, therefore need to follow conventions.

(A bracket labelled SENSE OF AUDIENCE *spans the STYLE/FORM, VOICE and STRUCTURE rows.)*

Three main areas to look for in folder checks:

1 Drafting
2 Punctuation
3 Grammar

1 Drafting skills
How are children using:
(a) paragraphs to structure a story;
(b) revision to add information, cut out unnecessary information, or re-order information;
(c) interesting titles;
(d) interesting lead sentences to capture the attention of an audience;
(e) repetition of words to give emphasis to the writing (Bang! Bang! and 'I ran and ran' etc.);
(f) the topic lists to select their topics for writing;
(g) editing skills for their writing;
(h) the short method of dating work, e.g. 11.7.81;
(i) the technique of brainstorming to list a variety of topics and lead sentences in order to give the *best* choice?

2 Punctuation

How are children using:

(a) capital letters for names of people (proper nouns), sentences beginning with a capital letter, a title of a piece of writing begins with a capital letter;

(b) 'talking' marks (quotation marks);

(c) commas to break a sentence into phrases;

(d) exclamation marks to show a certain kind of expression;

(e) apostrophes to show ownership/possession;

(f) apostrophes for omission/contractions;

(g) conjunctions or joining words to form a longer sentence from two small sentences;

(h) three dots to show a sentence is unfinished;

(i) a comma to separate lists of things (series);

(j) brackets to add extra detail to a sentence;

(k) abbreviations; and

(l) paragraphs?

3 Grammar

How are children using:

(a) tense;

(b) the subject and verb (they must agree, e.g. 'I am', *not* 'I are');

(c) similies which give the reader/audience a better picture, e.g. as swift as a deer;

(d) adverbs/adjectives which give a reader more description;

(e) phrases which make a sentence more interesting;

(f) prepositions which begin a phrase;

(g) words to replace weaker vocabulary;

(h) analogies to give impact?

Teacher's record

Below are two sample records from Reservoir East Primary School. The teacher's record is kept in conjunction with each pupil's writing folder. It would be passed on to the pupil's new teacher at the end of the year.

NAME: YEAR/LEVEL:

WRITING PROCESS	Date:						
Knowledge of language organization (surface structure) Pictorial representation							
Scribble writing							
Random invented letters							
Linear invented writing							
Strings of repetitive alphabetic letters							
Strings of varied alphabetic letters							
Groups of letters with space between							
Copying sentences or words unrelated to stated topic							
Any recognizable word (own)							
Developing knowledge of sound/symbol correspondences							
Any simple sentence							
Message quality (deep structure) Identifies objects in picture							
One sentence description of picture							
Tells a story about picture							
Has a concept that a message is conveyed (Tells message but what is written is not message)							
Correlation between story read back and piece of writing							
Correct (or near) words interspersed in right places							
Part of directional pattern is known — start top left move left to right return down left							

Reversal of directional pattern						
Correct directional pattern						
Correct directional pattern and spaces between words						

NAME: YEAR/LEVEL:

	Date:					
LANGUAGE						
Organization (surface structure) Correct spatial relations between letters, size, position						
Confident attitude towards attempted spelling						
Shows sound/symbol relationships in spelling — initial letters final letters medial letters						
Attempts to use resources to assist spelling						
Self-identification of spelling errors						
Use of upper and lower case letters in relevant places						
Attempt at punctuation						
Use of correct punctuation — capitals, fullstops question/exclamation marks talking marks, commas						
Story of two or more sentences						
Punctuated story of two or more sentences						
Message quality (deep structure) Writing approximates conventional form and child matches more or less what message says.						
Repetitive independent use of sentences						

Understands concept of a story						
Can retell own experiences in writing						
Can sequence events						
Expresses need to improve or rewrite (i.e. 2nd draft)						
Prepared to attempt editing for pages of a book						
Prepared to evaluate own stories against each other to select best one for publication						
Directional principles Extensive text without any difficulties of arrangement and spacing						

4 Writing record

This is kept in the child's writing folder. Each child completes the conference, small teaching group and publishing group sections. The teacher completes the folder check section.

The purpose of the record is so the teacher can monitor a writer's attendance at conferences, number and subjects of small teaching groups, attendance at publishing conferences and how often the writing folder has been checked.

A sample writing record follows on the next page.

My writing record   Sheet number . . .

Name

Room

Level

Conferences	Date
1	
2	
3	
4	
5	

The child completes this section after attending a writing conference. The title of the piece is recorded with the draft no. and the date of conference.

Small teaching groups

1

2

3

4

5

The child completes this section after attending a small teaching group. The subject and date of the group are recorded.

Publishing conferences

1

2

3

4

5

The teacher completes this section when checking drafts of a completed piece of writing. Any comments about the child's folder or lists and the date of folder check are recorded.

Folder check

1

2

3

4

5

The child completes this section after attending a polishing *or* pre-publishing conference. The title of the piece of writing worked on is recorded; and the date.

5 'Title Tally'

The purpose of the 'Title Tally' is to have a composite list of all completed pieces of writing available within the classroom. This list is pinned on a display board in the classroom.

The tally is helpful to the teacher in two ways:

1 It indicates the children's interests.
2 It indicates changes in titles from first drafts to publication.

Children also find the 'Title Tally' helpful. A title from this list may suggest a possible topic for other children to write about or may be inspiration in selecting a powerful title. (See sample on following page.)

6 Class collections

All completed pieces are typed in duplicate. One copy of the story is added to the class collection, which is bound. This serves as a permanent record of completed works and is also used as a take-home book.

The second copy becomes the author's own copy — to be used however the author deems fit. Many of the authors decide to cut up these copies and present them as books (in their own time and with the help perhaps of friends and family). These also become books for the class library.

In addition to these books, some stories are occasionally chosen to become class publications. In this case a publication team is elected. The children spend one week in school time, with the help of art and specialist teachers, producing a book to be added to the class library. (See Publication, page 25.)

7 Word banks/class lists

These consist of class combined lists of high-frequency words and topics and individual 'have-a-go' spelling cards. See spelling section (page 61) for samples.

TITLE TALLY

Writer	Draft Title	Published Title	Date Completed
Mick	Knightsie's Life	—	16·7·'82
Alisha	When I fell off my sister's horse	Ouch!	19·7·'82
Jason	When my mum's boyfriend got run over	The Upset.	19·7·'82
Raymond	Building my cubby house	Watch Out!	21·7·'82
Angelo	The Tapping Noise	Tap! Tap!	26·7·'82
Mark	When I went fishing	Flathead	26·7·'82
Kevin	Collingwood v's Hawthorn	The Weak Woodsmen	27·7·'82
Andrew	Car racing at Calder	They're Off!	2·8·'82
Sue	Going to Swan Hill	Journey Up	2·8·'82

Writing Development

Writing development can be traced through different dimensions. Listed below are four kinds of re-writing.[2]

1 Random drafting

These children write successive drafts without looking back to earlier drafts.

There is no comparison or weighing of options.

Changes between drafts seem arbitrary.

Rewriting is an exclusively forward motion.

Drafts more closely resemble a child at play than an adult at craft.

The decision to write, the composing and completing of a selection may all occur in the space of ten to fifteen minutes.

The concept of the work as a message, usage at another place and time, is not necessarily understood by the child.

These children do not reread with the intention of re-writing.

2 Refining

Rewriting means refining what they have already written.

These children may copy a piece over and over. They may change spellings, neaten handwriting, add a few lines, but their subject and voice are determined by the first draft.

Writing is not seen as a process of discovery.

Rewriting is a backwards motion of refining a draft.

They rarely cross out sections of their paper, insert lines with codes, or use arrows to move paragraphs.

Revision is usually in the form of adding information at the beginning or end of a selection, seldom does it occur in the interior of the text.

Content and structure of the piece remains the same. Refinement is only of minor consequence. (There are some changes in spelling and/or punctuation.)

3 Transition

The children move between periods when they refine drafts and periods when they abandon drafts, continually beginning new ones.

They sometimes appear to be 'random drafters', but they are closer to being 'refiners'.

Like 'refiners', these children can look back to assess and refine old drafts. But unlike 'refiners', they are not content with their earlier drafts.

When 'transition' children abandon old drafts and begin new ones, they show a restlessness which may lead them to become 'interacters'. (This restlessness seems to result from having higher standards for themselves.)

They can add information to the interior of the text.

4 Interacting

For these children revision results from interaction between writer and draft, between writer and internalized audience, between writer and evolving subject.

These children re-read to see what they have said and to discover what they want to say.

There is a constant vying between intended meaning and discovered meaning — between the forward notion of making and the backward motion of assessing.

There is an ability to shift between reader and writer, between critic and creator.

These children may make major re-organizations.

They can see information as temporary; moving *toward* meaning.

Their first drafts are of a higher quality; decisions about changes are made earlier.

2. Adapted from Graves, D. H., 'Patterns of Child Control of Process' in Walshe, R. D. (ed.), *Donald Graves in Australia*, pp.23-28, and Calkins, L., 'Children's Rewriting Strategies', published paper of the Writing Process Laboratory, Morill Hal., University of New Hampshire, pp.5-22

There are noticeable features of a child's writing which indicate at which stage they may be in their writing development.[3]

Writing as play

- There is no planning or goal.
- Writing, like play is present tense.
- There is no delay before a child writes. There is no deliberation over topic choice, layout, drawing, and words.
- Writing usually ends abruptly.
- The child may put emphasis into writing for the play of it rather than for the sake of communication. They may darken important words or put them in capitals.
- The child's writing is egocentric.
- The child writes in simple sentences, without dialogue or supporting information or exclamations.

Indicators of growth

- Ability to plan ahead.
- Use of resources.
- Use of conventions.
- Experimentation.
- Awareness of distant audience.
- Detail and precision.

Writing as craft

- The writing is no longer all present.
- There is a purpose in the writing.
- The child writes to communicate, and to perform.
- The child is able to plan and make use of other resources.
- The child shows flexibility and control of time and space.
- The child no longer writes solely for him or herself.
- The child uses a variety of punctuation.

3. Calkins, L., 'Children learn the Writer's Craft' in Walshe, op. cit., p.65 and 'When Children want to Punctuate: Basic Skills Belong in Context', ibid., p.89

Evaluation

The evaluation of writing should indicate to:

1 the child how effectively she or he is communicating;
2 the teacher the needs of the student for diagnosing and advising;
3 the parents how much progress the child is making;
4 all parties how effectively the program and materials reach their objectives.

Are the students developing as writers/communicators?[4]

1 **Look for growth in the use of conventions:**
   (This is often an early sign that children regard writing as an entity after the writing process is finished.)
   (a) Is there a concern about correctness?
   (b) Does the child want the paper to be legible?

2 **Look for awareness of a distant audience:**
   (a) Does the child write to communicate?
   (b) Does the child write to perform?
   (c) Does the child try to choose exciting story topics, use dialogue, and/or exclamation marks?
   (d) Does the child anticipate audience response and needs?

3 **Look for experimentation:**
   (a) Does the child try out rules?
   (b) Does the child experiment with the formalities of print (e.g. using onomatopoeic words such as 'Boom!' and 'Ouch!')
   (c) Does the child try out different editing devices?
   (d) Does the child revise in different ways?
   (e) Does the child attempt to integrate new information with old?

4. Calkins in Walshe, op. cit., pp.65-72

4 Look for use of resources:
(a) Does the child make use of reference books?
(b) Can he/she list information?
(c) Can she/he interview?
(d) Can he/she take notes?
(e) Can she/he report?

5 Look for ability to plan ahead:
(a) Does the child share his/her plans for a piece of writing?
(b) Are these plans realistic or appropriate?

A guide for evaluating writing[5]

1 Content
(a) Does the paper demonstrate independent thinking? Are the ideas original or merely borrowed from elsewhere?
(b) Does the writer have a controlling idea or purpose? Is that idea or purpose always clear, or is the reader sometimes unsure of how the material is intended to be taken?
(c) Are ideas clearly defined and fully developed? Does the writer explore the subject in depth, considering implications and possibilities, or is the thinking superficial?
(d) Is there enough specific information, and is that information more than just common knowledge?

2 Point of view
Is the writer's manner appropriate to the audience and purpose?

3 Organization
(a) Is the paper coherent? Would it be easier to follow if some of the material were re-arranged? Is there any unnecessary material?
(b) Is the material in the most effective order? Do the most important points get sufficient emphasis? Do lesser points get too much emphasis?
(c) Are individual paragraphs unified, coherent, and fully developed?

4 Style
(a) Can the writer vary the lengths and types of sentences to avoid monotony and achieve special emphasis?
(b) Are the writer's words precise and distinctive, or do they tend to be vague, trite, or bland?

5 Mechanics
To what extent do errors in grammar, spelling, or punctuation detract from the readability and authority of the paper?

6 Degree of difficulty
How ambitious is the paper? Has the writer attempted something difficult, or played it safe?

---

5. Murray, Donald M., 'A Guide for Evaluating Essays' in *English Journal*, 69, March, 1980

6 SPELLING IN THE WRITING CLASSROOM

Learning to spell is one aspect of learning to write. The aim of any spelling program should be to help children become confident, competent writers.[1]

Spelling is Developmental

All children go through certain stages on their way to becoming confident, competent spellers. There are stages in that development where the teacher should not consider children's attempts to spell as being either 'right' or 'wrong'. The teacher must make the children feel confident at each stage so that they are prepared to experiment for themselves.

There is *continuous* development in spelling; the 'stages' are not fixed or discrete. In fact, one piece of writing may show attempted spellings which slot into more than one stage.

We have chosen to adopt the stages as described by Gentry (1982)[2]. Bolton and Snowball (1985)[3] also use Gentry's stages. Their book gives a useful outline of the stages with plenty of examples and a complete chapter is devoted to activities which are relevant at each stage. The following descriptions are adapted from their book.

1 Precommunicative stage

(a) At this stage, the writing is not readable by others.
(b) There may be random strings of symbols (letters, numbers, or invented symbols).
(c) Letters may be in upper and lower case and used indiscriminantly.
(d) There is no indication of any knowledge of letter-sound correspondence.

---

1. *The Teaching of Spelling*, Education Department of Victoria, 1984, p.5
2. Gentry, J., An Analysis of Developmental Spelling in GNYS AT WRK, *The Reading Teacher*, 36, 2, 1982
3. Bolton, F. & Snowball, D., *Springboards: Ideas for Spelling*, Thomas Nelson, 1985

2 Semiphonetic stage

(a) Spelling at this stage is characterized by first attempts at letter-sound correspondence. It may be abbreviated, with only one or two letters (usually consonants) to represent a word, e.g. WK (walk), PO (piano), and S (saw).

(b) At this stage, children have great difficulty with vowels, e.g. FESH (fish).

(c) The writing may display spaces between words.

3 Phonetic spelling stage

(a) At this stage, the spelling is not standard, but the writing is meaningful and can usually be read by others.

(b) All essential sounds may be represented by letters, e.g. STIK (stick), TABL (table) and FLOR (floor).

(c) There may be substitution of incorrect letters with similar (or even the same) pronunciation. Actually, these substitutions often indicate that a great deal of common sense is being used by the speller, e.g. JRINK (drink) and CHRAIN (train).

(d) Nasal consonants may be omitted, e.g. STAP (stamp) and WET (went).

(e) Past tense may be represented in different ways, according to the sounds heard, e.g. PILD (peeled), LOOKT (looked) and TRADID (traded).

(f) Word segmentation and spatial orientation are clearly evident.

4 Transitional spelling stage

(a) Writers may operate within the transitional stage for a long period of time and during this stage, visual and morphemic strategies become more important.

(b) Vowels appear in every syllable, e.g. ELAFUNT.

(c) Nasals appear before consonants, e.g. COMBD.

(d) A vowel is inserted before a final 'r', e.g. RUNNUR instead of RUNNR.

(e) Common English letter sequences are used, e.g. YOUNITED.

(f) Vowel digraphs often appear, e.g. MAIK and MAYK.

(g) Inflectional endings (s, 's, ing, ed, est) are spelt conventionally.

(h) Correct letters may be used but in the incorrect sequence, e.g. BECUASE (because) and PLIAN (plain).

(i) Learned words (those spelled correctly) generally appear more often.

5 Correct spelling stage

(a) At this stage, knowledge of the English orthographic system is firmly established. Most of the words the speller wants to write are spelled correctly.

(b) The speller can often recognize when a word doesn't look right and can experiment with alternatives.

(c) A large reservoir of words is spelled automatically.

It must be emphasized that these 'stages' are continuous and over-lapping, and that one piece of writing may show attempted spellings at various stages, e.g.

Hi CaFe

Hi   Cathy

Wr hpvill a Br Bcu.

We're   having   a   barbecue.

lov From Paul.

Love   from   Paul

The words used here fit into the phonetic, transitional *and* correct stages.

Necessary Conditions for Learning to Spell

The teacher must aim to help children become aware of words and to develop their interest in words. An interest in word meanings and word structures is essential for a positive attitude to spelling. Such an attitude is more important than learning isolated words, as it encourages them to attempt spellings or to 'have a go'. Until children are prepared to 'have a go', there is little the teacher can do to help.

It is important for the teacher to continue confidence building by showing children that everyone makes mistakes and that there is an opportunity to correct them. If too much emphasis is placed on correct spelling initially, then writing will be crippled. It is also important that the teacher relays the message to the child that correct spelling is an attainable goal.

Important points:
1 The child must be shown the word in print and at the same time, hear it pronounced.
2 The child must be given time to fix it in her or his mind before having to write it.
3 The child should be encouraged to visualize the word from the 'image' in his or her head.
4 The word needs to be written often:
   (a) on the child's 'have-a-go' card;
   (b) in the child's first letter dictionary;
   (c) on wall charts or word lists;
   (d) in class books (e.g. topic book, book of spells, etc.)
Letting the child have a go first can save time because the word may be right.

Each child's own spelling dictionary, which they produce, should be freely available for others.

Spelling Strategies

Teachers must be concerned with equipping children with strategies that will enable them to attempt words they wish to spell, not with particular lists of words. They must draw the attention of children to *all* available strategies.

To consider the strategies, look at the word groups below (it is a listing for mature spellers) and think about how you would attempt to spell such words.

Group 1 *Visual memory*	Group 2 *Sound symbol correspondences*	Group 3 *Morphemic knowledge*
Ayatollah	asclepiadaceous	dissatisfied
Khomeiny	syzygy	disapprobation
fuchsia	coloxolyn	unnecessary
diarrhoea	myrmidon	unforgettable
Gerulaitis	crematistic	mediterranean

If you were asked to spell the above words, the responses might be:

Group 1 'I know what the word means, I'm familiar with it — I'll just jot something down to see if it *looks* right.'

Group 2 'What did you say? Say it again; say it slowly. What does it mean?'

Group 3 'Dissatisfied . . . now is that one 's' or two at the beginning?'

Group 1 words may be in your oral vocabulary and you may be very familiar with them, but you know that 'sounding them out' won't help because you are aware that there are unfamiliar letter patterns relating to the sounds you hear. You write the word down and look at it because you need to rely on visual memory. You know you've seen the words in the newspaper, on television, or in the environment.

Group 2 words may not be in your oral vocabulary and you may not be familiar with them in any form. The only thing you can do is to try to sound the word out bit by bit. You will not have seen the words often (or not at all) and you know you cannot rely on visual memory.

Group 3 words are usually familiar. Any uncertainties about spelling are usually best attended to by considering the parts ('units of meaning' or morphemes), e.g. in dissatisfied, one s is needed for the prefix *dis* and a second 's' is needed for the base word. However, in 'disapprobation', only one 's' is needed for the prefix. One may find it easier to remember the spelling of 'mediterranean' if it is known that the parts mean 'in the middle of/the land/the sea'.

Words can be divided into units of meaning (morphemes) as well as units of sound, and children who have the opportunity to compare words with related units of meaning can learn the conventions associated with their use, e.g. using morphemic knowledge, children will be able to make many words from the base word port:

re		s
im		er
ex	**port**	ed
trans		ing
de		ation

These three spelling strategies, visual memory, sound/symbol correspondences and morphemic knowledge, operate simultaneously. All three may help spell a single word. However, often one strategy may be more useful for spelling a particular word than the others. For example, the word categories above (1, 2 and 3) were chosen to demonstrate, in the best way possible, the three strategies.

With many words you can see which strategy will be the best in helping the child remember the correct spelling. With some words, two or more strategies will be helpful. Children need to be *taught* this. Let them in on the secret, spelling is not meant to be a mystery!

Gimmicks

Gimmicks are also useful in helping children remember correct spellings. Gimmicks are fun to play with, to invent and to share, e.g. 'A *pie*ce of *pie*', 'The princi*pal* is my *pal*'.

There are many well-known gimmicks, but all of us use our own to remember the spellings of certain words. These gimmicks are personal and will mean nothing to others (whereas strategies are universally applicable). Children have great fun inventing their own gimmicks and a useful practice is to keep a class gimmick book.

Which Words?

There is a variety of published lists. They have been compiled in many ways, but often for particular year levels. They are also supposed to be 'sequential'.

The lists are numerous because no single list has been widely applicable or suitable for all children of the same age. Neither have they been appropriate even for children of similar spelling ability. A further complication is that there are too many words in the English language from which to choose.

Of great significance is the fact that there has been no evidence to show that words taught from lists transfer to the writing situation. Clearly, that situation has been 'back to front'. The writing must determine the spelling needs. A *personal concern* for spelling words must be developed, and it is much more likely to occur when the individual child wishes to express words in his or her writing. **The need to spell is only obvious within the writing context, that is, it is only required when one wishes to write.**

Words *will* need to be recorded. Those that are recorded are mainly generated through experiences, interests and themes or topics. Others will be 'high frequency' words. The lists below provide a useful guide for creating individual, group or even class lists.

How to Devise Spelling Lists

1 Interest words
(a) Class —
  • longest/shortest words
  • 'sound' words
  • from literature
  • 'demons'
  • words we like
(b) Personal —
  • family
  • 'demons'
  • pets

2 Topic words
(a) Class —
  • social studies
  • science
  • shared experiences
(b) Personal —
  • projects
  • 'expert' areas

3 High frequency words

- maths terminology
- 'Dolch-type' words
- from room (e.g. labels)
- alternatives (e.g. other words for *said*)

4 Lists to extend vocabulary

- alternatives (e.g. other words for *walk*)
- base words (e.g. 'Port' words, see p. 60)
- descriptive words
- onomatopoeic words (e.g. thud, whoosh, buzz)

5 Word families

- same sound, same letter(s) (e.g. black, quack, smack)
- same sound, different letter(s) (e.g. key, sea, people)
- different sound, same letter(s) (e.g. bough, through, trough)
- word building

Organization

Developing an effective spelling program as part of a broader writing program is largely an organizational issue.

Teachers do need to know *how* to help children with spelling, but unless there are definite routines to follow, the many opportunities to attend to spelling will be missed.

Therefore, in order to have spelling occur as an integral part of the writing program, some decisions about what procedures will be followed need to be made. It is appropriate to include children in making such decisions. The children:

1 need to know that they are very much involved in the setting of the spelling procedures
2 must be familiar with the procedures
3 must take responsibility for 'working the system'.

This is important because the children must know that they are learning to spell, despite the absence of 'grade lists' and spelling drill (The chart, 'Am I Becoming A Good Speller' is useful in any classroom. A reduced version is shown on page 66 — P.E.T.A., 1983.) Children must

also know what to do when they can't spell a word they want to use in their writing and how to check spellings they have attempted.

Certain spelling procedures determined by the teacher and the children will apply to the whole class. However, the teacher will also negotiate with individual children to set up procedures which suit their individual needs. For example, all children might be required to attend to the spelling in every piece prior to publication. However, child A may be required to try all words she or he is uncertain of on a 'have-a-go' card but child B may be required to try only, say, five words on a 'have-a-go' card (with the teacher or the 'editorial committee' helping with the rest).

The procedures adopted will be those which suit best the teacher and the children in a particular class. However, the following ideas have proved successful in many 'writing classrooms' and are worthy of consideration.

'Have-a-Go' cards

Early writers usually only attempt to spell a word they are having trouble with. The correct form of the word is written in the final column by the teacher, parent, or spelling 'expert'.

Word banks (class and/or individual)

Here are two storage ideas:

index cards

labelled tins

Topic lists/books

These are often linked to social studies, science, or children's literature.

Word walls/charts

These are usually displayed and used for reference and to check 'Have-a-Go' cards. They are added to by individual children.

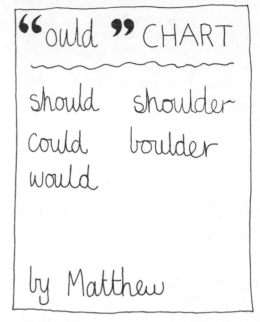

"ould" CHART

should   shoulder
could   boulder
would

by Matthew

When the chart no longer needs to be displayed, it can be added to a ring-bound book.

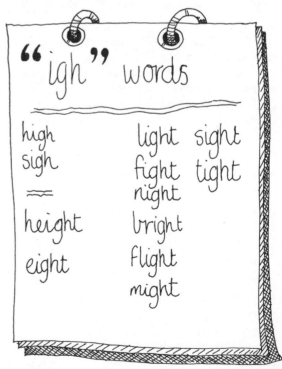

"igh" words

high   light   sight
sigh   fight   tight
——   night
height   bright
eight   flight
            might

Dictionaries

As well as class and individual dictionaries it is important that children have access to, and use, a wide range of published dictionaries.

Books in this format (i.e. with flaps) help the 'look-over-write-check' procedure. This develops visual memory of spelling patterns.

Books of word meanings develop the meanings of words and word parts. This includes prefixes, suffixes, compound words and contractions.

Spelling 'books'

These develop the children's knowledge of relationships between sounds and letters.

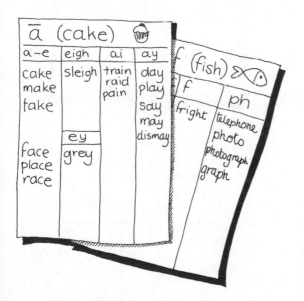

Sample pages for a child's spelling book.

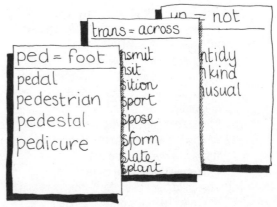

Spelling Procedures

Many of the preceding ideas will often be linked into procedures that children will follow. Two procedures are outlined below as a guide for teachers.

Procedure 1

1 Writing
   ↕ Revising
   Rewriting

2 The child proof-reads the draft when it is ready for publication.
   Correct spelling aids communication to the audience.

3 Circle or underline any suspected spelling errors.

4 (a) Take out a 'Have-a-Go' card.
   (b) Write the word as you think it is spelt.
   (c) Try several spellings.
   (d) Which looks right?
   (e) Check with teacher or another speller.

5 *If correct* the child writes the correct spelling in his or her writing draft and proceeds.

   If incorrect:
   (a) Child gets the class dictionary *Book of 'Spells'*.
   (b) The teacher writes the correct spelling in the dictionary and the child copies it into his or her own word bank.
   (c) Child and teacher talk about the word. Its difficult parts, the sound of word, its visual structure, tricks to remember, its meaning.
   (d) The teacher covers the word. The child writes the word from memory in his or her *word book* (using the look-cover-write-check method).
   (e) The child then uses the correct spelling of the word in the draft and continues.

4 (a) Have-a-Go card

5 (a) Class *Book of 'Spells'*
       Words are written in alphabetical order, a page for each letter. The book is left at Writing Materials Centre.

5 (b) The front half is a dictionary. The back half contains personal lists of words:
       (i)   like visual structure
       (ii) like meaning
       (iii) antonyms
       (iv) sounds etc.

Procedure 2

This procedure is more 'structured' but should still be negotiated with certain children so that it suits their needs.

1 Children use 'Have-a-Go' cards with a certain number of columns and lines, e.g.:
   (a) Years 5-6 = 4 columns, 15 lines
   (b) Years 1-3 = 3 columns, 8 lines

2 When the third column (filled in by the teacher, parent or tutor) is complete, it is cut off. The child makes a second copy of what is now a personal spelling list.

3 The strip from the original card can be cut up into word cards (for games, word banks, word sorts, etc.)
   The second strip can be pasted into a book with flaps for the look-cover-write-check routine.
   Individual word cards can also be used to commence word families if certain children benefit from repeated spelling patterns or clusters.

4 When individual children have spent time working with their words and are confident they know them, they can indicate that they are ready to be 'tested'.
   One way of indicating readiness for testing is to place the personal spelling list on a clip board for testing, or to have children hang their names on a display board.

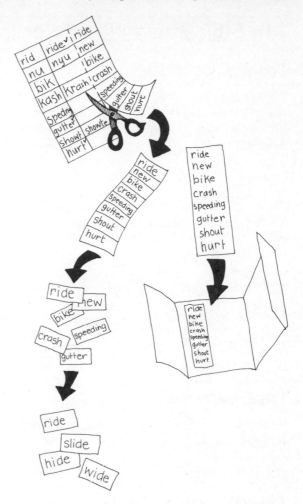

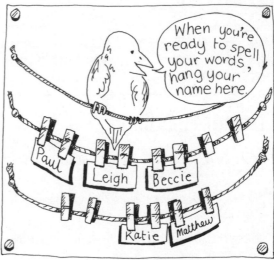

Am I Becoming a Good Speller?   Very likely you are, if you can say . . .

I *care* about spelling

I will need spelling all the time I am at school. My parents want me to be a good speller. When I leave school, people will expect me to spell well.

I *write* often

The more I write, the more I am practising spelling. I may not stop to check a spelling as I write my first draft, but I always check when I revise the draft.

I *proof-read* my writing

I finally proof-read any writing I will pass to readers. In doing this, I inspect every letter and all punctuation. Sometimes I also get a partner to check my 'proofing'.

I *read* every day

Reading leaves impressions of spelling in my mind. It also adds to the number of words I may use. While reading, I sometimes pause to notice spellings.

I *explore* words

For example, I notice letter-patterns like *tion, ough, qu*. And prefixes (like *dis*-) and suffixes (like -*less*). And meaning stems, as in para*graph*, bio*graph*y, tele*graph*ic.

I *check* to be sure

Sometimes while writing I ask for the spelling of a word. But I know that the final way to settle a doubt about a spelling is to consult a dictionary.

I *learn* new spellings

1 Look at the new word and say it softly.
2 Cover it and try to 'see' it in the mind.
3 Write it from memory.
4 Check (and if incorrect, repeat the four steps).

N.B. There are many other spelling ideas worth trying, such as . . .

- Keep adding to a personal list of 'Words I Have Learned to Spell'.
- Find and play spelling and language games that you enjoy.
- Keep improving your handwriting, because that will help your spelling.
- Try out ever spelling idea your teacher shows you and make a habit of any that work well for you, e.g. working with a partner.[4]

---

4. Primary English Teaching Association, Publications Editor — R. D. Walshe

---

Further Reading

Bolton, F. & Snowball, D., *Springboards: Ideas for Spelling*, Nelson, 1985.

Clay, M., *What Did I Write?* Heinemann Educational Books, 1975.

Education Department of South Australia, 'Spelling: R-7', *Language Arts*, Publications Branch, 1984.

Fehring, H. & Thomas, V., *The Teaching of Spelling*, Education Department of Victoria, 1984.
(Check the bibliography of this text for additional references.)

Hudson, C. & O'Toole, M., *Spelling — a teacher's guide*, Landmark Press, 1983.

Peters, M., *Spelling: Caught or Taught?*, Routledge & Kegan Paul, 1967.

Torbe, M., *Teaching Spelling*, (Revised edition), Ward Lock Educational, 1978.

7 READING AND THE WRITING PROGRAM

The Inter-dependence of Reading and Writing

Reading and writing are inter-dependent processes — necessary to one another and mutually beneficial for one another.[1]

Although it is possible to read without writing, it is an impossibility to write without reading. When teachers observe children writing, they see the children constantly reading and re-reading. The relationships between writing and reading are well documented by Shanklin.[2] She describes the following relationships:

1 Writing and reading are both constructive processes.

When writing, the writer composes, thereby **constructing** his or her own meaning. When reading, the reader **re-constructs** (comprehends) the author's meaning.

The use of terminology such as constructing and re-constructing helps to reinforce the inter-dependent nature of reading and writing. They are reciprocal processes and much is learned from one about the other.

2 While writing and reading, construction and re-construction, respectively, develop and change.

Although it has been commonly accepted for sometime that reconstruction during reading develops and changes, it is only now that researchers have also accepted that construction of meaning changes during writing. A common belief about writing has been that the author knows what she or he wants to say *before* writing it down, and this is partly true. However, what the author means often develops *during* the writing process as the author plays with his or her ideas. In many ways, 'writ-

1. Holt, S. & Vacca, J., 'Reading with a Sense of Writer: Writing with a Sense of Reader', *Language Arts*, 58, 8, 1981, p.937
2. Shanklin, N., *Relating Reading and Writing: Developing a Transactional Theory of the Writing Process*, Monograph in Language and Reading Studies, School of Education, Indiana University, 1981

ing finds its own meaning'. Many of us have had the experience of setting out to write a particular essay, only to find that, as a result of writing (and of the research, reading, exploration and thinking involved), we have come to new understandings, insights or meanings. Sometimes, the thrust of the essay turns out to be quite different from the original intention. The original plan may have been abandoned during writing, and the essay taken off in a completely new direction, or it may have been substantially re-ordered. This happens precisely because the construction of meaning *develops and changes during writing*.

3 Both writing and reading are dynamic processes, providing constant feedback.

When reading, predictions are confirmed or rejected so that readers build in their own feedback and check on comprehension. The same happens during writing. Authors must read the text already generated and make predictions about what should come next. As they read the text they detect 'errors'.

What has already been written places constraints upon what can be written next. The meaning that develops depends upon the relationships between all the words to one another. One *must* read prior text to continue writing.

4 Both writing and reading are developmental processes.

Learning to write and to read are developmental processes. The development is from gradual approximations to conventionally correct practice, and work at all stages is accepted.

'Reading readiness' practices have often intruded upon the natural learning that will occur when teachers understand the principles of developmental learning. 'Reading readiness' practices have often interrupted the process that can happen naturally for children who live in a literate society.

Recent research and practice have shown that the same is true for writing. Children who live in a literate society will learn to write naturally if given the opportunities to do so and they do *not* need 'writing readiness' tasks.

Very often, such 'readiness' tasks have kept children away from written language by occupying them with rows of clowns, geometric patterns, pictures with mistakes to find, or 'odd one out' exercises: The list could go on ad nauseum.

Holdaway[3] lists the following characteristics of developmental learning:

(a) It occurs 'naturally' in an environment in which the mature skill is being used by people with obvious functional success.

(b) It allows for gradual approximations towards final accomplishments. It begins with the learner role-playing him or herself as a user of the skill.

(c) It is supported by sympathetic, interactive adults who praise often and punish very seldom. Correction is positively presented only for 'mistakes' which are inappropriate to the stage of development. It occurs in a most secure social environment, resonant of optimism for the learner's ultimate success.

(d) It is constantly clarified by clear relationships to a total, meaningful environment of people and things — it is clamped tightly to sensory experience.

(e) It is self-programmed and self-paced. Massive self-motivated practice and repetition occur on self-selected items or sequences which the learner is determined to master.

These characteristics of learning prevail when young children learn to master oral language, which is an enormous feat. (Refer also to Cambourne, 1985.) These same conditions can operate within the classroom.

Implications for Instructional Practice

Since writing and reading are interdependent in many ways, they should share many instructional practices.

---

3. Holdaway, D., *Independence in Reading*, Ashton Scholastic, 2nd ed., 1980, p.14

Stotsky[4] found in her review of research that reading experience seems to be a consistent correlate of, or influence on, writing ability. She concluded that 'reading experience may be as critical a factor in developing writing ability as writing instruction itself'.

In practice, children show the observant teacher that many activities within the classroom do not separate writing and reading. The level of a child's comprehension skill can be determined by listening to the questions she or he asks about someone else's piece of writing. A teacher can learn of a child's ability to make inferences by listening to his or her reconstruction of meaning that has not been stated explicitly by the writer. And one way to learn about the purposes of reading is to write. 'Writing is, after all, the means by which reading material has come to be.'[5]

In many classroom activities, such as wall stories, shared book experience, directed reading-thinking activities, cloze activities, and so on, the teacher should always be ready to make points about both reading and writing.

Whether children are focusing on reading or writing, they will gain insights about both, e.g. when children are struggling in their writing with the spelling of a word, they are also gaining insights about word attack that will help them with their reading.

Questions children ask during writing conferences reflect their method of attacking meaning, e.g. 'What do you mean when you say . . .?' 'Could you read that part again?' 'What happened when . . .?' 'Tell us more about . . .'.

These kinds of questions help the writer understand what the reader looks for when approaching written material. These same kinds of questions are also asked during reading conferences. Calkins[6] describes classrooms where the questions asked during writing conferences are almost the same as those asked during reading conferences. She also reports teachers who have found that 'the more children interact with their reading, the better they do in their writing.'[7]

Writing sessions help the teacher and children in other ways too. During the writing session, areas of interest become more apparent and this makes it easier to refer children to reading material which will interest them. This advantage is particularly important when trying to interest the 'reluctant' reader. Choice of material is crucial for such a reader.

Writing sessions also help greater understanding of children's literature. Because the children struggle daily with word usage, ways of saying things, topic choice, and titles etc., they are more able to empathize with other authors — be they writers of stories, poetry, novels, or whatever.

When the children are involved in publishing their own work, they become more understanding of such issues as the interrelationship between text and illustrations. Children realize that illustrations add information and detail and that text and pictures are, in fact, important partners in presenting a total message.

Common Reading Activities

Their place in the writing program

One way of assessing how reading is catered for through children's writing is by taking a look at those reading activities which would be fundamental to most classrooms. We can then pinpoint when these reading activities are actually taking place in writing workshop sessions.

Now by breaking down the writing process into three stages (pre-writing, writing, post-writing), activities of specific concern to reading development can be planned by the teacher.

---

4. Stotsky, S., 'Research on Reading/Writing Relationships: A Synthesis and Suggested Directions', *Language Arts*, 60, 5, 1983, p.677
5. Holt, S. & Vacca, J., p.938

6. Calkins, L., *Lessons from a Child*, Heinemann, 1983
7. ibid., p.158

Common reading activities	Where in writing workshops activities occur
Reading: • of serial stories • of poetry • of short stories • of plays • for information • by the teacher (modelling)	• pre-writing (rehearsal) activities
Children's oral reading of their own stories (in draft form and in published form)	• pre-writing activities • writing conferences • share time
Reading comprehension (main idea, significant details, sequencing of events, etc.)	• as children write their drafts • as they revise/edit • writing conferences
Functional reading (reference skills, library skills, study skills)	• as children read books related to their own writing topic • as children pursue information to include in their writing
Silent reading of children's writing	• publishing conferences • share time
Reading for interest	• as children regularly borrow books from the school and class libraries

Writing	Reading opportunities and activities
Pre-writing (rehearsal)	• poetry reading • oral reading of stories in draft and published form • short story reading • play reading • activities such as extending children's sentences • cloze activities • 'read-a-long' taped stories

Writing	• children's oral reading of their drafts to themselves and in conferences
	• silent reading during composition of drafts to:
	  1 check meaning;
	  2 remind oneself of where the writing has been and where it should go;
	  3 regain momentum;
	  4 provide a 'breathing space', or even to avoid writing.
	• researching books for material for stories
	• functional reading and the development of reference, library and study skills
	• reading aloud to check sense, to hear the 'sound' of the language

Post-writing	• oral reading first to publishing conference group, then for audience response • silent reading of own and other children's published stories • borrowing books from class and school libraries • choosing to re-read a favorite book/story • reading and performing plays written by children

Teacher-scribing: Writing for Oneself

Language-experience and writing: complementary programs

Traditionally the language-experience approach focused on the teaching of reading, using the language of the children. As such, it was really a *reading-experience* approach. Speaking and listening were also attended to, but there was little, if any, writing done by the child.

The typical reading-experience approach takes the language generated orally by the child, and this is scribed by the teacher who then provides it as text for reading. Since it has been composed orally by the child/children, it is syntactically and semantically predictable for the reader. If further contextual cues are provided by using pictures, diagrams and so on, then the only 'unknown' component of the language which the child must attend to is the graphic component. The known components of language are used to unlock the one unknown component.

This is the rationale behind the language-experience approach and the reason why it has been so successful. (The language-experience approach was not just another bandwagon. Teachers have seen the benefits of such an approach and many of its procedures will continue to be used.)

However, there is a dilemma for the teacher who feels that it is important to expect the children to *write for themselves*, but who also feels that the modelling which scribing allows is also important. Such modelling allows the children to:

1 associate the meaning with print (not just pictures);
2 learn about directional conventions;
3 develop concepts about print components (e.g. letters, spaces, words);
4 learn about correct letter formations and different print styles;
5 develop an understanding of punctuation conventions;
6 realize that the same word is always spelled the same way.

Be aware that an over-emphasis on scribing can interfere with the children's spontaneous attempts to write. If scribing is at the expense of the children's endeavours, it can interfere with their willingness to explore writing.

Children might compare their first writing attempts with the teacher's conventional writing and infer that theirs is 'not good enough', 'babyish' or, worse still, not 'writing' at all. A child will compare several aspects of his or her writing and measure these against the teacher's. This may include:

1 handwriting ('I don't know how to write those letters', 'My letters don't look right' or 'I can't write quickly enough');
2 spelling ('I don't know how to spell yet', 'We haven't learned that word yet' or 'I can't use that word because I don't know how it's spelt').

A child may decide that it is much easier just to get the teacher to write whatever it is that she or he wants in print, and will not bother with the task her or himself. Also, if a child happens to dictate to a scribe using a different form of language than the one she or he would normally use in speech, and his or her reading material is therefore in this special ('different') form, then the language could become 'bookish' or stereotyped. When the child is later asked to write, the 'bookish' result will not truly be her or his own (in the sense that the child will not identify with it in the same way). In current terminology, the child will not 'own' it; it will not have her or his 'voice'.

Teachers may prefer to model writing behaviour during shared writing activities (such as wall stories), rather than individually. Some teachers find it useful to scribe for one small group of children one day a week, but require the children to write for themselves on the other four days.

How Do Children Perceive Written Language?

We think of the alphabetic principle as a wonderful invention BUTWEOVERLOOKANINVENTIONALMOSTASBRILLIANTANDCERTAINLYMORESIMPLE — namely the visual display of the lexical system as distinctive, perceptual units through the device of spaces. Indeed, written language is perceived as words, not as a series of individual letters.[8]

In written language, word boundaries are marked by spaces. However, word boundaries are not easily distinguished in oral language. In fact, there are often no boundaries between spoken words at all, e.g. 'djavagoodweegend' (Did you have a good weekend?) and 'apastate' (half-past eight).

Sometimes boundaries are placed incorrectly by early writers, e.g. 'wuns a pon a time' (once upon a time). This difficulty that children have with the concept of words has obvious consequences in their first attempts at writing, and is one explanation for the strings of letters observed and the words running into one another. (Occasionally, too, a child may recognize that words do exist as separate units, but may not see the need, at that point in time, to be bothered with leaving spaces!)

Words, in written language, *are* important and the teacher must do everything possible to develop the word concept and help children learn about words and how they work. The teacher must not only start with a focus on whole, meaningful language (sentence level at least) but also with a concern for words. Children need to be able to focus on words or be able to *attend to the word* level in written language. When learning how to read, they must get beyond the stage which Marie Clay calls 'creative inventing' (reading back an approximation of the message) to the stage where they can match the words they are saying with the actual words they are looking at.

In addition, the graphic representation of

---

8. Holdaway, D., *The Foundations of Literacy*, Ashton Scholastic, 1979, p.83

language (the 'unknown' component of language for the beginning reader/writer) includes the orthographic identity of the word. This refers to the correct pattern of letters within the printed word, and consequently the spelling of the word and the 'look' of it.

Reading and writing tasks which relate to the children's experience and backgrounds of knowledge, and which focus on the meaning the children are endeavouring to construct or re-construct, enable the children to use everything they already know about language to unlock what they don't know. That is, the known information is used to construct the unknown. (And it is a basic educational premise that we work from the known to the unknown.)

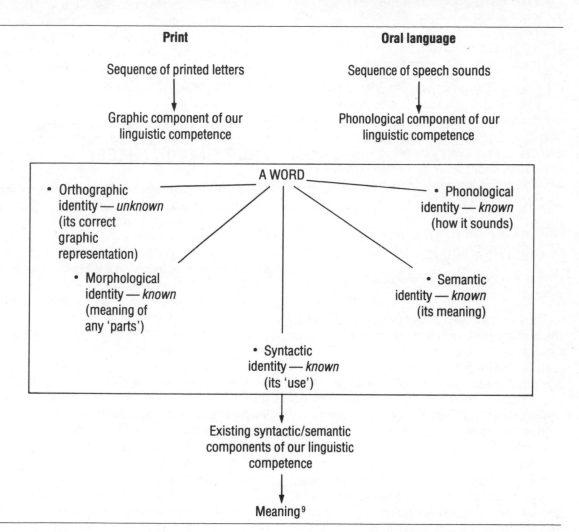

9. Adapted from Ehri, L., 'Beginning Reading from a Psycholinguistic Perspective: amalgamation of word identities', in Murray, F. (ed.), *The Recognition of Words*, International Reading Association, 1978

What do children know about words?

Consider a 'story' that a child has just produced orally. What does the child know about each of the words she or he has just used?

1 How it **sounds** (its phonological identity)
2 Its **meaning** (its semantic identity)
3 How it is **used** in the sentence (its syntactic identity)
4 The meaning of any 'parts', e.g. jump*s*/jump*ing*/jump*ed* (its morphological identity)

Possibly, the only thing the child can't do, is to write down, in conventional form, each of the words, i.e. the child may *not* know the correct graphic form of the word (its orthographic identity, 'ortho' simply meaning 'correct').

The teacher's task is to help children use what they know to enable them to learn about what they don't yet know.

Children who have a basic command of oral language know:

1 how to use language meaningfully;
2 how to use language for various purposes.

They also know many of the word's identities (how it sounds, how it is used in a sentence, what it means, etc.).

In a 'process approach' to writing, children are encouraged to write for themselves. At an early stage in their development, they may still be working out where the 'boundaries' of written words are and will certainly be inventing spellings before they know the conventional, correct spellings.

To experiment with and invent spellings, young children need to be particularly vocal. They can be heard sounding over and over again any particular word they wish to use. They repeat the sound of the word, or the sounds within it, as they try to represent those sounds with written symbols. In other words, at a very early stage in writing they must experiment with and develop knowledge about sound-symbol correspondences.

Therefore early writers *must* learn about letters. If we want them to progress beyond the stages of scribbling and strings of unrelated letters to invented spellings, then they must have opportunities for coming to terms with the symbols used to represent the sounds.

Note that they have already mastered the sounds. We don't have to teach sounds! We have to help them to learn about the letters and letter combinations which represent those sounds. (This is the 'reverse' of traditional phonics teaching where a teacher introduced a letter and taught the corresponding sound — as if the sounds weren't already known!)

Reading, Writing and the Role of the Teacher

In Chapter 7 an overview of the relationships between reading and writing is given. Information about these relationships is now substantial.

When attending to either reading or writing, the teacher must focus on the whole, meaningful language of children. This is the only language which will provide a useful framework from within which to work.

While reading, children need to attend to words as well as overall meaning. They will often have to attend to initial letters or letter clusters to aid their prediction of what a word might be. When this is done within the total language context, the attention to individual words or letters can be most successful.

While writing and attending to invented spellings, children need to represent the sounds they want with appropriate letters.

Consequently, in both reading and writing sessions, while the teacher must focus on meaningful language, she or he must also respond to children's questions and statements about words and letters in ways that will help them understand more about the nature of written language.

Further Reading

Butler, A. & Turbill, J., *Towards a Reading-Writing Classroom*, P.E.T.A., 1984.

Cambourne, 1985.
 'Language, Learning and Literacy' in Butler, A. & Turbill, J., *Towards a Reading/Writing Classroom*, P.E.T.A., 1984.

Goodman, K., Smith, B. & Meredith, R., *Language and Thinking in Schools*, Holt, Rinehart & Winston, 1976.

Harste, J., Burke, C. & Woodward, V., *Initial Encounters with Print: the Pragmatics of Written Language and Learning*, N.I.E. (Washington D.C.), U.S. Dept. of Edn., 1980-81.

Hopkins, H., *From Talkers to Readers the Natural Way*, Ashton Scholastic, 1977.

Pulvertaft, A., *Carry on Reading*, Ashton Scholastic, 1978.

8 THE PLACE OF LITERATURE IN THE WRITING PROGRAM

A major advantage of sharing literature with children is that it provides them with an extended range of language models. When children enjoy and respond to literature, it acts as a major impetus for writing as it develops their awareness of language use and form, of style and mood, and their vocabulary. It stirs their imagination and expands their reservoir of knowledge. As children hear and read models of prose and types of poetry, they can be stimulated to write their own stories and poems. Literature can lead to the creation of group experience charts, individual experience stories and group books.

Style is the quality which makes a piece of writing distinctive and individual. Exposure to various writing styles in literature develops the children's ability to adapt language to their own ideas. When analysing style, children should be alerted to certain techniques used by writers. Studying different styles provides numerous examples of writing in different moods and employing different techniques. The concern is not for the children to develop set techniques or styles but to have them realize that style changes according to the content, the purpose of the writing, the mood, and the author. Children learn that different authors have different styles just as they have.

Children who are readers, write differently. Children who are writers, read differently.

Good quality children's literature is an essential ingredient for having children become readers. Many children learn to read, but they do not become readers, that is, they do not *choose* to read unless literature has touched their lives in a special way. They may read Level 6, Book 2 now and Level 6, Book 3 next week because the teacher requires them to do so. But if these children are not choosing to read or re-read stories, poems, or plays for their own enjoyment, then we cannot call them readers and we, as teachers, have failed.

The main intention should always be that children enjoy literature; that they be excited by it, that they laugh hilariously, that they cry when it is sad. Literature should never be seen as supplementary reading, but rather as the *core* of the reading program.

While the major purpose of reading literature to children and of encouraging them to read it is to have them enjoy it and respond in a personal way, it cannot be assumed that children will become aware of writing styles or of the creative use of language techniques without some direct guidance by the teacher. Teachers will need to carefully intervene to ensure that desired 'connections' are made. For example, a chart of interesting words, descriptive phrases, and word pictures from literature can be kept. The teacher can alert children before a story is read to listen for the interesting way an author describes a particular person or object, or for words which describe a person's action, etc.

The teacher's role in developing an awareness and appreciation of literature can often be met during the 'introductory activity', as the focus for these activities is very often taken from literature (e.g. one week the focus might be tall stories, the next week, titles written by Ruth Park, followed by Ezra Jack Keats' complementary use of text and illustration).

An excellent reference for literary skills and literary forms which are appropriate at the various year levels is *Into Books*, (Thomas and Perry, 1984.)

Further Reading

Education Department of Victoria, *Happily Ever After*, 1975.

Holdaway, D., *The Foundations of Literacy*, Ashton Scholastic, 1979.

Hornsby, D., Sukarna, D. & Parry, J., *Read On: a Conference Approach to Reading*, Robert Andersen & Associates, 1986.

Sutherland, Z. & Arbuthnot, M., *Children and Books*, Scott Foresman & Co, 1977.

Thomas, R. & Perry, A., *Into Books*, Oxford University Press, 1984.

Walshe, R., Jensen, D. & Moore, T. (eds)., *Teaching Literature*, P.E.T.A., 1983.

9 A CONFERENCE APPROACH TO READING

The approach to writing described in this book is often called a 'conference approach' to writing, since the conference is the focal point of the program. Until teachers are attending to conference sessions with some degree of success, then what they are doing could not be called a process approach or conference approach to writing.

It is also possible to run a 'conference approach' to reading, and this approach will be outlined only briefly here. (It is the subject of another publication entitled *Read On: A Conference Approach to Reading* which details, amongst other things, examples of reading sessions based on literature conferences, planning done by teachers and 'units' of work based on particular authors or titles.)

A flowchart for a conference approach to reading is seen on the following page. The flowchart for the writing process is reproduced so that the two can be compared. The parallels are obvious.

Holdaway[1] is a most valuable reference. What Holdaway is describing in his book is basically a 'conference approach' to reading. However, Holdaway writes only about individual conferences with children, who are assumed to be reading different titles.

A recent trend in schools has been the use of multiple copies of paperback editions of good quality children's literature. Multiple copy sets make it possible for three or four children to read the one title at the same time. Since reading is mainly a 'solitary' occupation, we like to have the opportunity of sharing our impressions with someone who has read the same title. This is one reason why group conferences are useful. They can also be arranged when a group of children has read different titles by the same author. Such a conference would attend to issues about the author's style, the number of books the author has written, which are most

---

1. Holdaway, D., *Independence in Reading*, Ashton Scholastic, 2nd ed., 1980

popular, how the author's work compares with a different author's work, and so on. Group conferences can also be held when children have read books by different authors on the same topic or subject.

The steps which Holdaway outlines for the individual conference are also appropriate for group conferences. Additional comments regarding group conferences are made in the companion volume to this text.

The Teacher's Timetable

The following teacher's timetable has time allotments based on a session of approximately one hour or longer. This will obviously vary with year level and time available on any given day. With a prep. grade the 'Quiet Time' and 'Activity Time' may each only be of 10 minutes duration.

1 **Introductory activities** — 10-15 mins
   • Focus for week (this will often be a common focus for both the writing and reading workshops). (See pp. 9-15.)

2 **Quiet time** — 5-25 mins (depending on year level)
   • Silent reading (Teacher reading too!)

3 **Activity time** — 20-25 mins
   • Conferences (usually groups, sometimes individuals)
   • Activities related to reading
   • More silent reading (Children are free to continue reading silently if they wish — a major aim of our program is that they want and request to do this!)
   • Small-teaching groups.

4 **Share time** — 5-10 mins
   • Whole class together again for a discussion, display, performance or choral reading, etc.

Reading–Writing Connections

In a chapter with the title 'Reading–Writing Connections', Calkins writes:

> I was wrong to view two processes of reading and writing as separate. Wrong because writing involves reading, and because it reinforces and develops skills traditionally viewed as reading skills. And I was also wrong because writing can generate a stance toward reading which, regretfully, is rarely conveyed through reading programs.[2]

And later,

> Similarly, when children view themselves as authors, they approach texts with the consciousness of 'I am one who needs to know how texts are made.' Writing gives them a new reason to connect with reading.[3]

Many of the classroom teachers we work with have reported that, in time, the writing and reading conferences become more and more alike. Calkins reports similar findings, and lists some of the questions the children may be asking in reading conferences.[4] These, she notes, are almost the same as the questions the children may be asking in writing conferences.

The benefits for both the writing and reading sessions are many and include aspects of both learning and classroom organization. Children who read attend to writing in a different way, and children who write attend to reading in a different way. Insights from one profoundly affect the other. In addition, organizational procedures are the same and children have predictable routines to follow. (Compare the teacher's timetables for a writing workshop in Chapter 4 with the timetable suggested here for a reading session, pp. 35.)

Further Reading

Holdaway, D., *Independence in Reading*, Ashton Scholastic, 2nd Edition, 1980.

Hornsby, D., Sukarna, D. & Parry, J., *Read On: A Conference Approach to Reading*, Martin Educational, 1986.

2. Calkins, L., *Lessons from a Child*, Heinemann, 1983, p.155
3. ibid., p.157
4. ibid., p.158

Reading

Interests, abilities, experiences, ideas, needs, aspirations, hobbies.

Perhaps I could / I need to read about that?

Introductory activities
- listening
- discussing
- attending to a focus

- drawing
- note-making
- skimming and browsing
- checking library
- active seeking
- establishing difficulty
- establishing appropriateness

Focus (usually teacher-planned)
- Sharing enthusiasms about books
- Sharing knowledge about authors
- Teacher reading – poetry, songs, etc.
  - – fiction/non-fiction
  - – serial
- Teacher modelling

Reading
- Emphasis on:
  - whole books
  - real books
  - silent reading
  - understanding

- Setting purposes
- Comprehending
- Self-pacing in
  - interest
  - difficulty
  - speed
- Self-evaluation
  - personal satisfaction
  - skills
  - new interests
  - self correction
  - future need

Conferences
- making connections
- establishing themes in literature
- discussion of content/message
- oral reading to establish facts, support points of view
- re-construction of message (comprehension)
- attending to character, plot, setting, style, etc.

Small teaching groups
- skills practice
- oral reading, word identification, library skills, individual needs

Post-reading activities
- related reading
- creative response
  - writing
  - preparing for mime, drama, puppetry, etc.
  - art/craft
  - music
- audience reading

- study skills
  - topic studies
  - projects
  - research
- reading for life needs

Sharing
- oral reading
- performance
- debate
- display
- writing
- presentation
  - of project
  - of research
- interviewing

- discussion
  - insights
  - personal feelings
  - pleasure
  - empathy etc.
- learning centres to support reading in content areas

Writing

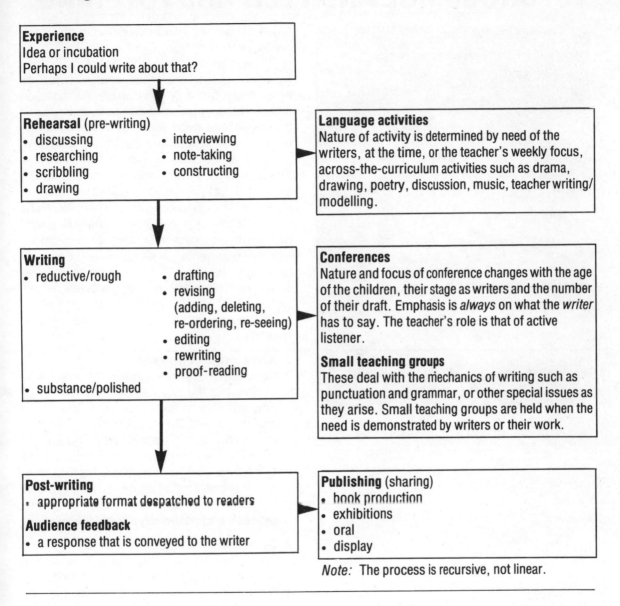

Experience
Idea or incubation
Perhaps I could write about that?

Rehearsal (pre-writing)
- discussing
- researching
- scribbling
- drawing
- interviewing
- note-taking
- constructing

Language activities
Nature of activity is determined by need of the writers, at the time, or the teacher's weekly focus, across-the-curriculum activities such as drama, drawing, poetry, discussion, music, teacher writing/modelling.

Writing
- reductive/rough
- drafting
- revising
  (adding, deleting, re-ordering, re-seeing)
- editing
- rewriting
- proof-reading
- substance/polished

Conferences
Nature and focus of conference changes with the age of the children, their stage as writers and the number of their draft. Emphasis is *always* on what the *writer* has to say. The teacher's role is that of active listener.

Small teaching groups
These deal with the mechanics of writing such as punctuation and grammar, or other special issues as they arise. Small teaching groups are held when the need is demonstrated by writers or their work.

Post-writing
- appropriate format despatched to readers

Audience feedback
- a response that is conveyed to the writer

Publishing (sharing)
- book production
- exhibitions
- oral
- display

Note: The process is recursive, not linear.

10 CROSS-AGE AND PEER-AGE TUTORING

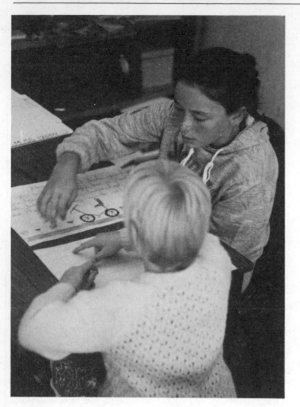

Much lip service has been given to these two areas, and many books and articles have been published expounding the benefits of both. However, getting them to function successfully in a classroom is another thing. All too often what tends to happen in these situations is that the most able child takes over and does the work or completes the task for the less able. When this happens, who benefits? The more able participant gets the reassurance that she or he is 'smart', and also is able to revise her or his skills. The child needing the help learns he or she needs help and doesn't really learn any new skills. At least, this was our experience when experimenting with cross- and peer-age tutoring before our 'writing classrooms' developed. But since the writing program began, tutoring has been very successful and beneficial. We believe it has worked for the following reasons:

1 Knowledge of process

Because the tutors themselves are totally involved in the program at their own level, they are able to fully understand their tasks and purposes. The predictability of the total program is easily transferred to the tutoring situation. As the tutors themselves have been through the process of learning skills within a conference situation, they are able to guide their 'student' through the same process and not simply supply the answers.

2 Selection of tutors

Anybody can be a tutor under the writing program system. All children are certain of their own skill area because of their growing lists of accomplishments in their writing folder ('Things I Can Do'). Peers are aware of who has certain skills around the classroom because of the sharing of folders. Because of this self-awareness, children often volunteer to help others or find themselves a tutor. Children see other children as resources and use each other as such. As a result of the folder lists, they are aware of each other's strengths and accept them readily.

3 Lack of stigma attached to needing tutoring

Because of the above reasons, there is no stigma attached to being tutored. Therefore, without the barriers of feeling 'dumb', work is covered quite quickly and well.

Where and When It Happens

Peer-age tutoring is a spontaneous occurrence. Children are free to move about during the writing session and so organize themselves. Cross-age tutoring, of course, needs to be timetabled. It can be arranged to suit the requirements of the classrooms involved. In order to minimize the movements between rooms, the older tutors can each develop a tutoring kit containing all the equipment they may need.

Cross-age tutors can also keep a tutoring diary where they record the names of children they work with and the areas in which they work. This will enable them to report back to the teachers and to decide to what degree the session has been successful. The tutors can sometimes have conference sessions with the teacher on this point, in order to plan subsequent sessions.

The diary reinforces the notion of control for the tutor. It is, in effect, their 'work program' and they share the responsibility of planning and evaluation.

Further Reading

Allen, Vernon L., *Children As Teachers: Theory And Research On Tutoring*, New York: Academic Press, 1976.

'Research On Children Tutoring Children: A Critical Review', *Review of Educational Research*, 46, 1976, pp. 355-385.

Ehly, Stewart W. & Larsen, Stephen C., *Peer Tutoring For Individualized Instruction*, Allyn & Bacon, Inc. Boston, Massachusetts, 1980.

Heibert, Elfrieda H., 'Peers As Reading Teachers', *Language Arts*, 57, 8, University of Kentucky, Lexington, Kentucky, Nov/Dec 1980, pp. 877-881.

The Tutor's Role at Different Stages of Writing

Pre-writing	• *Dialogue* — through talk, establish a child's expert areas — 'What do you know about . . .?' • Develop topic ideas. *Note:* Tutors may often be the 'key' to helping reluctant writers.

Writing	• One-to-one conferences — future drafts discussed.
	• Helps to
	  (a) highlight focus and main idea in the revision-drafting process;
	  (b) refine and change.
	• Helps solve individual problems in mechanics and spelling. Tutor may plan these sessions, e.g. word bank games for spelling; word family building.

Post-writing	• Tutors serve as the first 'outside' audience for children's completed pieces. • Actual guidance in terms of layout, illustrations etc. may also be given. • Cross-sharing of writing between grades through tutors.

APPENDIX

Writing Topics

This is *not* a suggested topic list but is provided as a guide to teachers about the sorts of experiences children choose to write about. All of the following topics were selected by the children in Years 2-6. They are arranged according to general topic areas. Where there are two titles, the first was the title of the draft and the second was the title of the published piece.

Accidents

My brother nearly got killed
The fire
The burn out

When I fell off my sister's horse/'Ouch!'
My cat got run over/'Meow, Meow'
When my mum's boyfriend got run over/'The upset'
When I went over my handlebars/'Prang!'
When my teeth were pulled out/'Fozzey's Fangs'
The day I smashed my bike
When I stuck a pitchfork in my eye
When I busted my head/When I split my head open
The day I fell out of the window
The day I was knocked out
The day I got a big bruise/'Smash'
When I went deaf
When I went away and cut my foot
When I was lost at the market/'Lost'
When I was stuck in the elevator
When a snake crawled over my leg
Stack
When I had a hernia
A bee stung me/'Oh!'
Stitch
Our Mercedes crashed

Holidays/Trips/Excursions

At the mountains
The cemetery
Going camping
The graveyard
When I went to the tip
Flash Gordon
On the holidays
Italy
The wedding
The best excursion
When I went to the restaurant
Mum — I'm cold
The trip to Phillip Island
The city
Tree tops
The day we nearly didn't go to the snow
Going swimming
The park
The trip
Best and fairest

When I went to Sydney/'Centrepoint'
When I went to my Grandpa's
When I went night rollerskating
Grade 6 camp/'Swan Hill'
A trip on a ferry/'Ship Ahoy'
When I went fishing/'Flathead'
When I went to South Melbourne/'Goal after Goal'
The day my family and I went to the park
When I went to Little Athletics
When we went to the farm in Grade Two
When I went to the zoo in Grade Three
When I went to the city in Grade Two
When I went to the snow
The day I went camping
My journey up to Swan Hill/'Journey Up!'
Port Macquarie
When I went to Strath Creek
Swan Hill/Swan Hill Tour
Camp Manyung
First day at Cowes
When I went to French Island
When I went to Adelaide
What a disaster!
Blow out, They're off/'They're off!'
The weak Woodsmen
The night I slept at my sisters
Healesville in Grade 5

Family/Birthdays/Home

Me and my dad and my brother play football
When my grandfather died
Playing in the garden
When my mum went to hospital
Shifting
My Communion
The visitors
There they are!
The birthday boy
That's Ace!

Happy Birthday!
When my dog had a pup/'My dog's first pup'
Cubby house/'Watch Out'
The day my family and I went to the park
When my mother went into hospital
When I baby-sat my cousin
When we got our swimming pool
'Curly' (a dog as a birthday present)
The day my brother was born
Tap! Tap! (incidents at home)
Fooled badly
Peppy
When I cleaned my Dad's car
When my sister found a cat
First year of education
Marvellous McEnroe
Hey Aliesha!

Personal (Achievement)

Chicken pox
When I saw the firecrackers
Cubs
Ballet
Football
The fight
The place I go
Brownies
Tap dancing
The dancing competition
The concert
When I had a hole in my heart
Shivers — it's my turn
Oh, no — it's my turn
And we're off

When I went swimming and got my 50-metres
    certificate
Cross country
Playing a Test
When I joined a footy club
The day I got my glasses
The day I got my horse
When I first met Miss Parry
The time I first started school
When I had my photo taken for the newspaper/
    'Click 2'
Ripper!
A First

Miscellaneous

The fireworks
Rex and Tash
Rugby
The black out
Kiss
Clay and art
The pigeon
Kiss in Melbourne
The earth tremor
The army
The dead pigeon
Star wars
Kitty
Leggo
Boring

Girls! Girls! Girls! (Poem)
Spooky Night/'A Night of Fright'
Frankenstein II
Hai-Yai!
Paul
Whoooo . . .!
Blazes
Bobby Dazzler (newspaper report)
Rope ladder — How to make
Water off a duck's back (Poem)

ANNOTATED BIBLIOGRAPHY

Selected Journal Articles

Atwell, Nancie, 'Writing and Reading Literature from the Inside Out', *Language Arts*, 61, 3, March 1984.
This article addresses the issue of reading/writing links and how teachers might get classrooms and schools to become literate environments. The author uses case studies of two Year 8 students to demonstrate her own practice in tackling the issue of reading/writing connections, and coping with 'conferences' through letter writing.

Bard, Therese Bissen, *Children's Response to Literature*, Educational Document 144034, July 1976.
The document considers many aspects of children's response to literature. Among the topics discussed are: factors within the child (related to age, sex and intelligence) that teachers and researchers agree may affect a child's enjoyment of literature; a research study on the relationship between story content and a child's psychological and developmental needs — books with animal characters, realistic picture story books for children in kindergarten and first grade, realistic and fantasy stories that may be read aloud to older children; aspects of literature (content, form and literary quality) that may affect response and elements of the environment (the teacher's own enjoyment, the classroom situation, teaching methods and parental influence) that affect a child's response to literature. The paper recommends numerous books that may be used in a literature program.

Blackburn, Ellen, 'Common Ground: Developing Relationships between Reading and Writing', *Language Arts*, 61, 4, April 1984.
In this article the principles of writing process are examined and those same principles applied to reading. The author emphasises that the common ground between the processes of reading and writing has to be prepared and cultivated by the teacher. Samples of work and discussion with Year 1 students make this article particularly useful to infant teachers.

Boomer, Garth, 'Towards a Model of the Composing Process in Writing', Paper presented at the ANZAAS Conference, Adelaide, May 1980.
This paper describes the composing process behind the teaching of writing. Teaching writing involves establishing and maintaining conditions conclusive to the act, diagnosing at what point, in what way and at what level to intervene in the process, and the framing of appropriate responses to the finished product. The article offers a map of useful points of entry or observation to the teacher.

Calkins, Lucy, 'Work in Progress: One School's Writing Program', National Elementary Principal V.59, 4, Atkinson School, New Hampshire, June 1980, pp. 34-38.
The article covers all children from Prep. to Grade six using the writing program. It offers practical suggestions and guidelines to use when teaching the writing process. Can be very helpful to teachers wanting ideas on how to get their children started on the program.

Calkins, Lucy, 'Heads Up: Write What You See', *Language Arts 55*, 3, 7th March, 1978, pp. 355.
This article describes how to get children started on a topic and includes practical suggestions on helping children choose a topic to write about. It suggests that children will write well only when they speak in their own voices about their own concerns.

Calkins, Lucy, 'Children Discover What Writers Know', *Learning V.* 6, 8, April 1978, Public School in Middlefield, Connecticut, pp. 34-7.
A teacher describes a technique for helping children discover what they want to write about and how to develop and expand an original idea. Questions put to the child to

help him or her to understand his or her own writing and the meaning the writer wishes to convey to the audience.

Calkins, Lucy, 'Children Write . . . and their Writing Becomes their Textbook', *Language Arts 55*, 6, October 1978, Centre School, Middlefield Connecticut, pp. 804-810.
The articles give many detailed examples of children's writings and how they can be taught to refine their writing skills. It describes the method of how teacher and child may work together through conferences and re-writing sessions to help improve the child's understanding of the writing process.

Calkins, Lucy, 'Learning to Throw Away', *Language Arts 56*, 7, University of New Hampshire, October, 1979, pp. 747-52.
This article works through the developmental stages of a fourth grader's writing as she learns to revise, rewrite and constantly change her stories.

Calkins, Lucy, 'Writers Need Readers Not Robins', *Language Arts 55*, 6,, September 1978, Center School, Middlefield, Connecticut, pp 704-7.
The article provides examples of how fourth grade students can help one another to improve the rough drafts of their compositions.

Cullinan, Bernice E. & Carmichael, Carolyn W. (eds.), 'Literature and Young Children', Educational Document 138 979, 1977.
A literature-based language program that puts emphasis on developing children's oral skills. Summary of ideas that teachers have found work with children. Lists many books to use in the program.

Dresser, Janet, 'Role Modeling in the Writing Process, Educational Document 03811, published paper from Writing Process Lab. Morrill Hall, University of New Hampshire.
A brief account of how a grade 3 teacher approached group conferences with her children.

Duncan, Patricia H. & McLeod, Alan M., 'The Development of Children's Composition following Targeted Discussions of a Distinctive Literature Selection', Educational Document 194882, December 1980.

A detailed study of the growth of seventh grade students' writing ability after a 'listen-discussion-write' teaching procedure was used, in which the students read a literature selection, asked and answered questions and wrote stories of their own. Preliminary analysis of the students writing samples appeared to confirm the 'listen-discuss-write' technique as a means of fostering the growths of writing skills for the participants.

Dyson, Anne Haas & Genishi Celia, 'Whatta Ya Tryin' to Write?': Writing as an Interactive Process', *Language Arts Vol. 59*, 2, February 1982, University of Georgia, Athens.
The article considers the questions: What are the purposes for which each beginning writer uses oral language when composing and how is the writing process of each child affected by social context? Describes a detailed study of two children and how their social interaction with their peers was used as a tool for encoding words into written form.

Edelsky, Carole & Smith, Karen, 'Is That Writing — or are those Marks just a Figment of your Curriculum?', *Language Arts 61*, 1, January 1984.
The article tackles the difficult issue of what is authentic or inauthentic writing. The authors use samples from one classroom which they describe as having a 'whole-language orientation'.

Egan, Judith E. 'Making Time for Writing', Educational Document 03811, Rockwell School, Atkinson, New Hampshire. Published paper from Writing Process Lab. Morrill Hall, University of New Hampshire.
A grade two teacher discusses the problem she faced in trying to fit more writing into a day which is already too short. Writing becomes her basis from which all other language arts concepts emerge. She describes a morning session in her class.

Giacobbe, Mary Ellen, 'How to Help Children Become More Responsible for Their Writing', Educational Document 03811, Atkinson Academy, Atkinson, N.H.. Published paper from Writing Process Lab. Morrill Hall, University of New Hampshire.

A brief account of how a grade one teacher conducts a conference with an individual writer. It describes how she records the child's progress, listing the skills she has acquired.

Graves, Donald H., 'We Won't Let Them Write', *Language Arts 54*, October, 1979, National Language Conference, Thornton, Victoria, pp. 817-24.
This article discusses the reasons for the lack of writing in the classroom. It stresses the crisis in writing in our community, where adults write even less than children and concludes with a number of aspects about particular teachers, where 'good' writers have been found to evident in the classrooms.

Graves, Donald H., 'Balance the Basics: Let Them Write', *Learning 6*, 8, April, 1978, pp. 30-3.
This details brief individual conferences between teacher and student during the course of writing which help the student to clarify his or her thinking on the topics. This improves skills and develops enthusiasm and pleasure in written communication.

Graves, Donald H., 'Andrea Learns To Make Writing Hard', *Language Arts 56*, 5, May 1979, University of New Hampshire, pp. 569-76.
A study of the development of a third grader's approach to writing and how she learns to revise, throw out and refine.

Graves, Donald H., 'Let Children Show us How to Help Them Write', *Visible Language 13*, 1, 1979, pp. 16-28.
This article presents findings from an indepth study of children's composing processes in an effort to explain handwriting performance in relation to child development and the writing process.

Graves, Donald H. & Calkins, Lucy, 'Research Update: Children Learn The Writers' Craft', *Language Arts 57*, 2, February, 1980, pp. 207-13.
This article follows the changes in children's writing from the first grade through to fourth grade, presenting case study data that show how children's writing shifts from play to draft.

Graves, Donald H., 'Research Update: Writing Research For the Eighties', *Language Arts 58*, 2, February 1981, pp. 197-206.
The article explores questions of concern for writing research in the areas of context in writing and the teaching of writing. It discusses some research designs and procedures.

Haley-James, Shirley M., 'Revising Writing in the Upper Grades', *Language Arts 58*, 5, May 1981, Reading Education at Georgia State University in Atlanta, pp. 562-566.
The article discusses when and how writing should be revised. It considers the questions: Who is the writing for? Why is the writing being done? Should this writing be revised at all? Such questions determine whether the writing is developed further or aborted, whether its presentation should be formal or informal, whether reader response should be sought or only the writer's on re-reading it.

Hannan, Elspeth & Hamilton, Gord., 'Writing: What to Look For, What to Do', *Language Arts 61*, 4, April 1984, pp. 364-366.
As the title suggests, this article gives samples of writing behaviour demonstrated by the child, what this indicates in terms of writing development and what the teacher might do to support and encourage the writer for further development. Appropriate for teachers at all levels in the primary school.

Hennings, Dorothy Grant, 'Literature, Language and Expression', Educational Document 124909, 1976, U.S.A.
Described in this paper are techniques for helping primary school children build writing skills by using literature selections as models for expression.

Howard, Patricia, 'Sharing — The Show and Tell of Writing', Educational Document 03811, Atkinson Academy, Atkinson, New Hampshire. Published paper from Writing Process Laboratory, Morrill Hall, University of New Hampshire.
A grade 5 teacher describes an activity within her writing sessions called 'sharing'. When the children 'share' they read their story or draft and ask for comments. Children and

teacher share ideas and help each other to become better writers.

Barbara Kamler, 'One Child, One Teacher, One Classroom. The Story or One Piece of Writing . . .', *Language Arts 57*, 6, September 1980, Atkinson School, New Hampshire, pp. 680-93.
A step-by-step account of how the classroom environment provided by a second grade teacher allowed one of her students to experience her own writing process and develop as a writer.

Klein, L. Marvin, 'Teaching Writing in the Elementary Grades', Elementary School Journal 81, 5, May 1981, Western Washington University, pp. 320-326.
The article identifies a number of known generalizations about writing and some specifics about children's writing. It points out the implications for what and how a teacher of children teaches written expression.

Reynolds, Helen, 'Getting Off the Mark . . . Day One', Educational Document 03811, Atkinson Academy, Atkinson, New Hampshire. Published Paper from Writing Process Laboratory, Morrill Hall, University of New Hampshire.
A teacher of first grade describes the first day when she introduces her children to the writing program.

Searle, Dennis & Dillon, David, 'Responding to Student Writing: What is Said and How It Is Said', *Language Arts 57*, 7, October 1980, University of Alberta, Edmonton, Alberta, Canada, pp 773-781.
The article argues that teachers should look more closely at the content or meaning of the children's writing rather than the form. It describes a framework for teachers to use when responding to children's writing and also discusses the treatment of mechanics in the writing process.

Smith, Lewis B., 'They Found A Golden Letter: Stories by Children', *Reading Teacher 29*, 6, March 1976, University of Idaho, Moscow, pp. 541-45.

This article describes a reading program developed in Lewiston, Idaho called 'Communication Skills Through Authorship' (C.S.T.A.). The program offers methods of dealing with children who are eager to express themselves. The students are able to tape their own stories for use by the entire class.

Tway, Eileen, 'Teacher Response to Children's Writing', *Language Arts 57*, 7, October 1980, Miami University, Oxford, Ohio, pp. 763-772.
The article describes ten carefully chosen children from McCuffey Laboratory School at Miami University, ranging in age from 6 to 11 years who showed talent and/or promise in their writing. It gives examples of their work and how the teacher responds to each according to their needs and level of writing development.

Tway, Eileen, 'Books for Canadian Kids: Children's Literature and Creative Writing', Educational Document 132566, 1976.
One of teacher's tasks is to help children to enjoy creative writing and to become effective in written communication. Literature may be read to inspire children to write, to help them explore their own imaginations, and to show the techniques used by authors in characterization and dramatization. Children may share stories they write, putting them into booklets and adding them to the class library.

Vukelich, Carol & Golden, Joanne, 'The Development of Writing In Young Children', *Childhood Education 57*, 3, Jan-Feb. 1981, College of Education, University of Delaware, Newmark, pp. 167-170.
This article reviews research findings on the development of writing skills in young children and identifies some implications for the classroom teacher.

Watson, Jerry J., 'Fine As Silk and Rough As Chapped Hands', *English Education 12*, 1, October 1980, pp.10-15.
The article discusses how well-written, moving children's stories can be used to promote children's own writings.

GENERAL FURTHER READING

Barnes, D., *From Communication to Curriculum*, Penguin, 1976.

Bissex, G., *GNYS AT WRK*, Harvard University Press, 1980.

Britton, J., *Language and Learning*, Pelican, 1970.

Graves, D., *A Researcher Learns to Write: Selected articles and monographs*, Heinemann, 1984.

Murray, D., *Learning by Teaching: Selected Articles on Writing and Teaching*, Boynton/Cook Pub. Inc., 1982.

Smith, F., *Writing and the Writer*, Heinemann, 1982.